Conversations with Women
The Journey Toward Self-Esteem

DEB PAVLICO MS, LPC

DEDICATION

This book is dedicated to all the women who have inspired me in my life, including the woman who refused to let me give up or give in, my biggest supporter and best friend, J.

ACKNOWLEDGMENTS

I would like to acknowledge the five women who agreed to take time and share their journeys with me. They were honest, supportive and genuine in their vulnerabilities and beautiful failings. Without their courage and dedication, this book would not be possible. I would also like to thank the women who responded to the questionnaire. Their insight and authenticity adds wonderful perspective to this topic. To my editor, Elizabeth Mohn, thank you for your intellectual comments and always providing feedback in a gentle way. You have a beautiful spirit. To my cousin Ann, thanks for the tip on the great editor. Finally, thanks to my mom for her support and encouragement.

CONTENTS

Introduction

I've missed more than 9000 shots in my career. I've lost almost 300 games. 26 times, I've been trusted to take the game winning shot and missed. I've failed over and over and over again in my life. And that is why I succeed.
-Michael Jordan

As a counselor, I have had an opportunity to sit across from some truly amazing clients. They are talented, intelligent, good mothers, good leaders, good students and more. But they don't believe they are amazing. As a matter of fact, many of them can only point out their failings. I found myself asking, how can very accomplished individuals feel they are not good enough; and think they have to continue to prove—to themselves and others—that they are good enough, strong enough, smart enough, or simply *enough?*

I didn't have to go too far for an answer because I was looking in the mirror at a younger version of myself. I had felt the same way at one time, actually for a very long time in my life. Feeling like I wasn't worthy enough to be in the same room with some people. People I was certain who were so much "better" than me.

When I started counseling college students it

became clear that something needed to be done. Young women who are top of their class, receiving athletic scholarships and making a positive impact on the college community were not feeling worthy of good relationships, good health or a good life. It seemed they were destined to be "me" or other women in their thirties, forties, and fifties who are amazing and deserving, yet drowning in their own self-doubt.

When it was just me having these self-esteem issues, I thought, "No big deal. I'm a big girl. I'll just put on that face, hope they don't notice and pretend I belong here." It took time to realize that I was worthy enough to be in any room. Not better or worse than anyone, just presenting my best me. I am glad that I have gotten here; however, for others to look at me as a role model for self-esteem, when I wasn't experiencing it, was a lie. If I'm truly a role model, I will tell you about my doubt and fears, and not make you think I don't have any. That would be unrealistic. I doubt often, but still in all things believe I am capable. Capable of ruling the world? No, but capable of ruling *my* world, my actions, my feelings.

I love stories, and I learn so much from observing people. As a matter of fact, because of technology, we seem to observe people more than ever before. We pick role models based on their personalities, their senses of humor, their style and their treatment of others. So, why not share some female role models for self-esteem? That is what I feel I've done in this book.

The women in this book have personally inspired me in so many ways. They are strong, smart, courageous, and amazing. Five women will be introduced in their own chapters, sharing their stories. Their stories teach us that self-esteem can be developed and that each woman has her own unique journey toward that goal. I also asked several other incredible women to participate by completing a questionnaire. Their responses are included in the Introspection sections and other sections of the book. They share their own definitions of self-esteem, their "aha" moments and their advice to others about how to improve self-esteem. 1 do hope these stories and comments will inspire you to actively grow your own self-esteem, to help those around you build theirs and to come to love and accept the amazing person you are.

Defining Self-Esteem

Always be a first-rate version of yourself, instead of a second-rate version of somebody else.
-Judy Garland

What is self-esteem? It seems like an easy question to answer, but have you ever tried to put words to it? If you think about the words "self-esteem," you can almost picture it, and then you might feel something. A feeling that says, "Yes, I have self-esteem," or "No, I don't really feel good about myself," or any number of combinations of thoughts and feelings. But if I were to ask you to define it, what would you say? What are the words?

Melissa W. says, "Self-esteem is how I view myself both physically and emotionally. My self-worth." Lacey T. defines self-esteem as "the way you think and feel about yourself." According to Ann P., "Self-esteem is confidence and pride in yourself." These are some great definitions. But, as I started with the interviews, the more we talked about self-esteem, the more confused the subject became. One woman suggested that you can't have too much self-esteem or you might be considered conceited. Another said she prefers to be humble and feels she isn't being true to that part of herself when she feels accomplished. The more we talked, the more there seemed to be a disparity between the words in the definition and what women truly felt, or wanted to feel inside. I wondered why, and after additional research I think I may have found an answer.

Self-Esteem is not Self-Conceit

Since I planned to have conversations with women about self-esteem, I thought it would be helpful to find a definition of the term. Aside from asking women to provide their own thoughts, I did some research and found several definitions. Some were good, and others were confusing and frustrating.

When looking for a definition I started at the place everybody would these days, the internet. Dictionaries online or otherwise are good sources of information, right? Here is what I found on Merriam-Webster's website: Self-esteem (1) a confidence and satisfaction in oneself: self-respect, (2) self-conceit.[1]

The first definition made sense to me. But self-conceit? Really? I decided that couldn't be right, so started to look at other resources. Another online dictionary had similar definitions: Self-esteem (1) a realistic respect for or favorable impression of oneself; self-respect, (2) an inordinately or exaggeratedly favorable impression of oneself.[2]

"Exaggeratedly favorable impression?" Additional dictionary searches were proving no better. The Collins English dictionary includes the definition of "an unduly high opinion of oneself; vanity,"[3] and the American English version states that self-esteem is "undue pride in oneself; conceit."[4]

Are you kidding me? So if I have self-worth or self-love I may also have self-conceit, vanity or an exaggerated impression of myself? Does this make sense to you? To further complicate matters, Merriam-Webster also included these synonyms and antonyms.

> **Synonyms:** *ego, pridefulness, self-regard, self-respect*
> **Antonyms:** *humbleness, humility, modesty*

"Ego," that is something that might have a negative connotation (e.g., egocentric, egotist, etc.). The antonyms are also confusing, inferring that if I have self-esteem I can't be humble, modest, or exercise humility. Could this be why we have such trouble developing self-esteem? These definitions indicate that if we develop self-esteem, we may be considered conceited or lacking modesty. In the interviews I presented this definition, and in some cases the woman's own interpretation indicated that you don't want to have too much self-esteem, or you may appear conceited.

What message are we sending with definitions such as these? Can you imagine a thirteen-year-old doing a report on self-esteem and finding these definitions? Does any thirteen-year-old, or anyone else for that matter, want to be conceited, vain or egotistical? Conceit is considered a negative attribute in our society and maybe for good reason. But, to compare it to or define it as self-esteem is wrong. I think it is possible to be humble and still feel worthy. I think you can be modest and still have self-respect.

It seems the above definitions are either erroneously defined, or over-defined. By erroneously defined I mean if you include self-worth and self-conceit, you should also include self-loathing. Self-worth or self-esteem can be the midway point between self-conceit (too much of a good thing) and self-loathing (too little of a good thing). Or, if we consider it over-defined, that means self-conceit doesn't apply at all. Isn't self-esteem simply a positive view of oneself? How one views oneself. Feeling positive about oneself, capable of one's abilities and worthy of love, acceptance and so on? It certainly can be confusing.

A Better Alternative to "Vanity"

Fortunately for all of us, there are other definitions out there that are more comprehensive and less judgmental. As a matter of fact, many different interpretations of self-esteem exist. Mruk and O'Brien indicated their research related to self-esteem revealed the body of work includes more than "8300 articles, chapters and books, and occurs in the title of over 17,200 works."[5] My research was not anywhere near that extensive. Below are a handful of alternatives to the dictionary versions.

The website psychology.about.com states that self-esteem is "used to describe a person's overall sense of self-worth or personal value." The website goes on to say that self-esteem usually includes ideas about oneself, including ideas about appearance, actions and behaviors. Also, one's self-esteem is usually seen as a character trait because it is long lasting. This website also identifies the synonyms for self-esteem to be "self-worth, self-respect, and self-value." Now those are synonyms I can believe in.

Mayo believes that self-esteem can lead others to respect you. Also, self-esteem allows people to view themselves accurately.[6] Now we're getting somewhere. This sounds like it's a healthy view of the self, being okay with who I am regardless of my flaws.

The dictionary versions that exclude self-loathing or low self-esteem indicate you have to be aware you don't have too much, but they don't help you understand that you can also have too little. In my role as a counselor, I see more people with low self-esteem than high self-esteem. Finding balance is the key in self-esteem, as in all other areas of our lives. As a matter of fact, healthy self-esteem can encourage us to feel worthy of, and seek balance in our lives. Nathanial Branden stated: "It's impossible to have too much self-esteem. People who are arrogant or boastful actually show a lack of self-esteem. Those who are truly comfortable with themselves and their achievements take pleasure in being who they are—they don't need to tell the world about it.[7] Not telling the world about "it" as Branden mentions seems in line with modesty to me. This, of course, contradicts self-esteem being defined as "self-conceit."

Pyszczynski and Kesebir[8] support the importance of understanding that self-esteem is not narcissism. Nor is it self-conceit. It may not be easily defined, but at least we should agree on what it is *not*. Removing self-conceit from the dictionary may not be possible in the short term, but we certainly don't have to support this definition in our life or the lives of those we touch. We need to treat self-esteem as a positive attribute and not something to be avoided or masked.

How Will We Define Self-Esteem?

After reviewing many options, Nathanial Branden seems to provide a worthwhile definition when he says: "Self-esteem has two interrelated aspects: it entails a sense of personal efficacy and a sense of personal worth. It is the integrated sum of self-confidence and self-respect. It is the conviction that one is competent to live and worthy of living."[9] I like the idea that self-esteem isn't only about recognizing that I am capable, but it is also about believing that I am worthy of everything I am capable of achieving.

Of course, there are also the personal definitions

provided by the women who completed the Self-Esteem Questionnaire including:

Believing and trusting in oneself and having the confidence to overcome life's challenges.
-Tammy G.

When you are sure of yourself. Confident!
-Ruth O.

I think self-esteem is thinking enough of yourself to take care of yourself (mind and body), treating yourself with respect, and also expecting to be treated by others with respect.
-Linda C.

Self-esteem to me is confidence, assurance in one's abilities including decision making. Making ideal choices which allow you to have honesty and integrity in the way you live your life.
-Janine O.

I define self-esteem as self-worth, how I value and respect myself and feeling confident with who I am. I try to avoid tying self-esteem to feeling good about accomplishments but I do believe self-esteem derives out of having direction and purpose in life. If you can't get focused, it is a floundering type of feeling that truly affects your self-esteem and how you value yourself. I define low self-esteem as being full of "self-doubt." Not believing you are capable.
-Diane F.

I suppose it's judging ourselves and our actions and determining our self-worth.
-Joanina L.

I define it as the impression that I have of myself, how I regard myself or the respect I have for myself.
-Christina D.

I would define self-esteem by the way you feel about yourself, emotionally, physically, and mentally. It is the way you carry yourself.
-Ashely W.

In looking at all these angles defining self-esteem, there is one note of importance. The most significant definition is the one *you* embrace. Will you define it as a positive and something to emulate with humility and confidence? Or will you retain that belief that too much self-esteem equals self-conceit? How do you want your children, siblings and friends to see themselves; as conceited, or as worthy and capable? I choose the latter.

My Journey

In every aspect of our lives, we are always asking
ourselves, How am I of value? What is my worth? Yet
I believe that worthiness is our birthright.
–Oprah Winfrey

Although I feel vulnerable sharing my story, I am excited for the possibility that it will help you with your journey. It's not easy to show this side of myself because I have always worried about what other people think. But, I have always been my own worst critic, and I have learned not to trust that criticism. Those critical thoughts have often been unhelpful, untrue and even unhealthy.

I consider myself "accomplished," and many people who know me would probably agree. But self-esteem isn't about accomplishments. If it were, it would come a lot more easily to people. My self-esteem has been impacted by that little voice inside that tells me that I am worthy, or that I am not. For years I believed the message "I'm not worthy." While reaching goals and collecting accomplishments I had been hard on myself as to my worthiness. I might say that it's just luck, or that it is a great opportunity someone gave me, or that I had a lot of help. It was so hard to accept that maybe I had accomplished something, and it was okay to admit it.

Let's be clear, I wasn't wearing poor self-esteem on my forehead. I didn't wake up every morning and say, "Wow, I have low self-esteem and should probably do something about that." The critical voice is almost subtle. It didn't say, "You don't deserve great things." Instead, it would always challenge any good I did. "Well, you're smart, but not as smart as...," "You're pretty, but not as pretty as ..." "Well, at least you have a 'good personality,' just not as good as..." Frankly, it was exhausting to constantly be in a battle with myself.

So, what is my story?

My parents' divorce became final before I was ten years old. The year was 1975, and women were not really getting divorced all that often. As a matter of fact, judgment could be harsh for women who divorced, and—at that time—women were still trying to define their place in the world. It was a time before anyone had heard of the glass ceiling, but if a woman had, she more likely would have wondered how to clean it, not break it. So I learned early on that women could be judged harshly for their actions.

In addition, money was pretty tight in our house. I think as a society we don't expect a lot from kids who grow up "poor." Because we don't expect much, we don't challenge them to expect it from themselves. It could be my perception, but the truth is I don't recall a teacher pulling me aside and asking why I wasn't working to my potential. There were no mentors reaching out to help me apply to college or for scholarships. I believe this experience added to my negative self-esteem and taught me to feel "less than" others.

It's not as though self-esteem knocked on my door and said, "Hey, you. You really don't feel worthy enough to live a great life, so get your act together or you'll be making decisions based on less than what you truly are capable of, and less than you believe is possible. You will make poor choices that limit you in your life, and all the decision you make will be based on a figment of your imagination." That's the rub. Our self-talk isn't always clear. When it is, some of us tend to accept it as truth instead of challenge it. That's what I did. Without even realizing it, I was accepting a belief that I was "less than."

I continued on to college and struggled with my major and my grades. My mother was determined that her daughters would not have to depend on a husband to take care of them, and so she felt that I needed a stable career path. So, I was guided to a degree in business. I wasn't happy. My own goal was to go to New York and become an actress. A stable career choice, right? Eventually I graduated with that business degree. Because of my poor grades, I had some trouble finding a job, but eventually that network—you know the one I created with my "great personality"—came through. A friend introduced me to a company I would stay with for the next thirteen years.

Regarding relationships, another belief I learned was that if I didn't have a partner, it proved that I was not a valuable or lovable person. So, as you might imagine, that led to unhealthy relationships in which I expected little and gave everything.

Fast forward to age thirty. I'm working six days a week in a Fortune 500 company. I was dedicated and driven to excel. What I was really driven to was to prove I was good enough—that I was worthy of being noticed. Over the next decade, I climbed that corporate ladder knowing my goal was to be vice president of something. It didn't matter what, but inside I knew when I achieved that, I would finally "feel" as though I had made it. I would then be "somebody," be "good." That was the biggest lie I ever told myself. Although I didn't intentionally lie, it was really more of a life philosophy that I held too tightly to. How often we hold onto old beliefs only to wake up one day and wonder why we didn't see through them sooner.

While I was working my way up in my day job, a friend and I opened a coffeehouse from the ground up. Why not? I was only working fifty hours a week during the day. Who needed nights and weekends for rest? Well, it turned out the coffeehouse was a wonderful experience, and I'm glad I did it. I know you hear stories about business partners never speaking again, but mine was a great guy who became one of my dearest friends. We sold the business a few years later after taking some losses. However, as I look back I can appreciate the many lessons learned and am still very proud of that accomplishment.

Life was moving forward, and I thought everything was going well. I did always have this gnawing feeling that something wasn't right, but I could never put my finger on it. And I never really stopped long enough to figure it out. Each job change or promotion brought on a new set of challenges and opportunities to learn. I dove in, wanting and needing to succeed at each task. Once I accomplished the task, I simply got bored and looked for the next opportunity.

Again, I wasn't really aware of my low self-esteem. That critical voice was just a part of me. I was living life and moving toward goals I thought I wanted. And like many other "driven" women, I was racking up accomplishments. So what happened next? My title changed to Vice President, but my feelings about myself didn't change. I expected a big parade, pats on the back from all my self-doubts saying "Atta girl! You finally made it. You can now feel as good as you are." But, that didn't happen. And that was a turning point. Up until then I hadn't stopped long enough to reflect on my life, my goals, my wants and my desires. I just plowed forward toward what I thought I wanted.

My Trifecta

At age forty, I was still accomplishing things left and right, joining organizations, volunteering, leading, planning and so on. I was about to get a wake-up call. There were three significant events that took place that year. Each contributed to shifting my own perspective about myself and prompted me to get out of my own way and come into the life I wanted and deserved.

Event 1:

I was eating dinner with friends, and, mid bite, I passed out, hit my head on the table and fell to the floor. A trip to the emergency room landed me in the heart hospital. WOW! The heart hospital. Tests were done, and fortunately my heart was fine, but my mind started working overtime. I'm sure you have heard a similar story before. Whenever we are faced with our own mortality, we begin to reflect on our lives. I started asking myself if I was happy. Asking if I had done those things in my life I wanted; if I felt fulfilled.

In some ways I was very blessed. In one major way, I was very unhappy. That was at work. I worked with some of the most amazing people that I had ever met. The company had been good to me for the thirteen years I was there. But when I went to the office I had a hollow feeling where my heart should be. Finally, I had achieved that vice president goal I set for myself. So why did I feel so unhappy, so unfulfilled? Why was it an effort to go into work?

Event 2:

I was having lunch with a colleague. I was again complaining that I needed a change. It was February, and I always hated February. That month seems to lend itself to being cold and dark. Like my mood at the time. As I continued complaining, my colleague looked at me across the table and said something along the lines of "You're not going anywhere. You'll still be here next February saying the same thing." Of course my first thought was, "How could she say such a thing? How could she be so blunt? Doesn't she see I just need to vent?" But, she was right. I had been having this conversation off and on for several years. And each February I was still there. It was as if she turned on a light in a dark room. I could finally see with clarity that the only person keeping me stuck was me.

Event 3:

I had always liked problem solving. The big picture puzzles and the small ones. I remember sitting with my boss going over some information I had compiled for the department. He looked at me as if impressed and asked "What's your IQ anyway?" I just smiled and we continued, but after I left that meeting something changed. See, no one had ever asked me what my IQ was. As a matter of fact, as far as smarts go, I was never considered to be the smart one in my family. That was my sister—who, by the way, is awesome and very smart.

I was forty years old, and—until that moment—I had never really allowed myself to feel *smart*. To this day I smile every time I think of it. Better still, I believe it to be true. Just for the record, I have no idea what my IQ is, but every day I do feel smart enough to handle what comes my way. I also believe we are all capable of being smart enough to make good decisions in our lives. At this point, I was starting to recognize and embrace my positive self-esteem.

So what would a smart person do? I was forty, unfulfilled in work and tired of hearing myself complain. I decided to not limit my "smart decisions" to my work life. It was time to be "smart" for myself.

A Time For Me

My next project was not work related, but "me" related. I stopped and took time to evaluate my life. Just as any project I had taken on before, I defined the problem, defined all possible solutions, and when choosing one, I identified the steps needed to achieve that goal. At the time, I didn't realize healthy self-esteem was one of my goals, but it certainly was one of the results.

As with any good project manager, I began with research. Knowing that I was unhappy in my life I bought two books, *Self Matters: Creating Your Life from the Inside Out*, by Dr. Phil McGraw and *Life's a Bitch and Then You Change Careers* by Andrea Kay. I read through and did the exercises in each and two things became clear to me. First, I needed a job where I "motivated and inspired" individuals. As I reflected on my career path, those jobs were the ones that most fulfilled me. Second, I was blaming a lot of people— none of whom were me—for my place in life. That was eye opening. I was blaming my mother for my not going to New York to pursue acting; I was blaming the school system for not helping me find a career path, and on and on.

When I realized that those beliefs might have been true twenty plus years ago, they were not true today. There was no one stopping me from moving to New York tomorrow. And no one but me was stopping me from going to school, changing careers, or accepting less than I deserved. I was the one who was at the crux of my problems.

Now I don't want to make this seem harder, or easier, than it was. At first I was overwhelmed with the role I was playing in my own life. Can you imagine? I was *surprised* at the role I played in *my* life. Over the years, I chose to play a less active role in my happiness than I wanted to admit. Reflecting on all those lost opportunities was a difficult, but necessary, task. It was frustrating, but at the same time empowering. For the first time I realized there wasn't a better, stronger, faster, or smarter version of "me" to wait for before making decisions about my life. I now felt free to depend on this version of me—not the one I was waiting for, whoever she was. This version had to make a choice. It was scary and exciting at the same time.

As I mentioned earlier, my life was pretty good, but this career piece, which is pretty big part of identity for me, had to change. I enrolled in a master's program for Community Counseling, starting with one class to see if that might be something I wanted to do. When I realized I wanted to pursue a career as a counselor I made another decision. I quit my job and attended class full time. I didn't want to spend another day dedicating time to something that didn't give me a sense of purpose. Besides, I wanted to "motivate and inspire" people. How could I inspire individuals to make changes if I wasn't willing to take risks in my own life?

For the record, thanks to a lucrative career and a supportive relationship I did have some money saved and the encouragement to quit my job. I couldn't afford to go out to dinner all the time, and I was still afraid of how it might all work out. But once I made the decision everything seemed to fall into place. I was awarded a graduate assistantship that further helped offset the costs. I studied hard, met some great people, graduated and began my new career. As a Licensed Professional Counselor I am so happy and finally feel as though I am living my destiny, not trying to find it. I also learned how to recognize the inner voice that served only to criticize me. If I had a friend who always criticized me, I would stop spending time with that person. I would consider that relationship unhealthy and unproductive. So, to recognize that I was being critical of myself, and to know I play the most significant role in *my* life, I began to question, and then challenge these beliefs. A few years later, life is wonderful.

Today, I feel free of the exhausting banter between my worthy self and the voice that always told me I wasn't good enough. Although I don't allow those negative thoughts to consume me anymore, that doesn't mean they don't try to pop up once in a while. Then, I have to challenge them with the truth. What is the truth? The truth is that anything that I have focused my attention on I have successfully completed, and I am worthy and capable of achieving anything I desire. Oh, and that's not self-conceit, just reality.

Ruth's Journey

Dream as if you'll live forever. Live as if you'll die today.
–James Dean

I met Ruth several years ago when I was starting a coffee business. She had a lot of energy and great ideas, and I really liked meeting her. Soon after, I saw her picture in the paper participating in community service work. It reminded me that I used to love volunteering and wanted to get back to those roots. I then joined the local Junior League and began spending more time with her and other amazing women. I appreciated and admired Ruth before I sat with her for this interview. Afterward, I am even more impressed with the woman she is. She is someone who inspires me to be more generous and giving, and to be an overall better person.

Deb: When we met, you had this public relations firm, and you're really smart and seem like you really have this great gift to be able to just do this. Nothing just comes, obviously we work at things, but I thought, "Wow, you really have your act together." So, you inspired me when I saw the picture in the paper [of you volunteering] to say, "She's doing this, and I want to aspire to be like this, so I'm going to do this." It brought me back to my roots of giving. It's helpful and makes us feel good.

Ruth: Well, it took me a long time to figure out what I was going to do first of all. When I first went to college I went for criminal justice, and I was going to be in the FBI. I finished a year and figured I didn't want to do that, and I went for paralegal and then for computers. It took me a while to figure out what I wanted to do, and I was very aimless. I liked a lot of things but just didn't know what I wanted to do. And I think it took me until I was about thirty to figure out that it was marketing. I was good at it. I just kind of knew I was good at it.

Deb: How did you get there?

Ruth: Work. I got divorced when my children were very young [ages 2 and 5]. Talk about self-doubt—my marriage failed. Although my ex-husband was not the best husband in the world, I blamed myself. I would think that I should have been different—there should have been more that I could do. I could be a better wife. And there was probably a year where I was just a wreck. I didn't think I was good enough for anybody. How could I be better to somebody, more attractive, a better mother? I went to work at a bank. I gave up my career to move with my husband and raise my kids. So I relocated to a different branch. Somebody there noticed I had a knack for computers, and I went back to school for that. I really enjoyed it because we weren't the generation where they taught it in school, and it was one of the best things I did because it made me an asset to any kind of job I wanted, especially in banking. Someone left for a new bank and took me with them to work as assistant to the district sales manager. There was a lot of marketing in that job, so I would travel to the branches and produce videos and do marketing materials, and I loved it. That was my first taste of what I really loved: marketing. And luckily the banks at that time paid for you to go to school. You could take a certain amount of credits and I took advantage of all of that. I moved around in some different positions and ended up working as the marketing director after a few different positions there. And then a friend of mine introduced me to the head of an advertising and marketing firm. They wanted to start up a PR firm and thought I would be a good person to go there and start their PR division.

Deb: Wow. So you were tapped for it.

Ruth: Yes.

Deb: And how were you feeling about yourself during this time?

Ruth: I was wondering, "Could I do it?" You know, I knew that I loved everything I was doing at the bank. I loved all the marketing. I loved the fact that they encouraged community involvement. That's where I really started getting involved in the community. They wanted you to participate in bowl-a-thons and walk-a-thons, and work at the soup kitchen. Because of my role in marketing I would be kind of the ring leader. I took my kids because I wanted them to be introduced to that world. I just really got involved in everything I could. Got involved in the Chamber [of Commerce], the United Way, and whatever I could get involved in. But when [a friend] approached me and introduced me to the owner [of the firm], I just doubted myself. "Can I really do this? I'm okay in this environment, but over there I'd be on my own." I would be the only person they would have trying to start up this division. So, I took a chance and I left. I went over there and did it. And started from the ground up: What kind of marketing materials do we need to go out and sell? I was a sales person first. I learned I loved to sell. I was very relaxed.

I went out with the owner a couple of times and brought on a couple PR clients and built that for them. I was there for about a year. I realized an ad agency was too slow paced for me. It's not so customer focused, but more like, "This is what I think you should have, and you need to listen to us because we are the experts." I'm kind of a little different that way. I ask, "What do you want?" and I want to make what you want work with whatever tools I can. My children were in school, and I also needed more flexibility in my schedule. My son was playing basketball and my daughter was playing basketball and soccer, and I wanted to be able to go to the games after school. So I left and took a chance. At that time I was engaged to [my fiancé], and we had a wedding planned. I took a chance, and I was going to leave with no health insurance or anything and start up my own company. And, fortunately, one of the larger companies I brought on came with me. So when I left. . .

Deb: You had a client.

Ruth: Yes, so I sent out some goofy marketing materials and brought on a [entertainment industry] client, which was a huge client because they had me doing PR and marketing for all these shows at a time when business was booming for them because the economy was better. The person who was in charge of development there was someone I knew from my banking days. I was amazed at the time. I was scared to death, but amazed that, "Wow, this was really happening."

Deb: It seems like everything was aligned.

Ruth: It just kind of happened. I think the best thing I ever did for myself was getting so involved when I was in banking, getting so involved with so many organizations and meeting so many people. Because it's all about the contacts you have, and I think that's what gives you that comfort level. Because I'm still insecure. You wouldn't know it. Like I look at you, and I wouldn't think you were. I'm a member of a women's executive group, and the first time they asked me [to participate], I said, "No, look at the people who are here. They're all wealthy. They're all in major companies." Well, the second year they came back to me and said, "We really want you so think about it."

I'm still uncomfortable when I'm there because I think they look at me as a novelty because I'm so different from them. I didn't come from the same background. When I first got divorced, I had no money. Fortunately my parents helped me pay for daycare so I could work. I worked part time at night and full time during the day. I started a basket business because I needed extra money for Christmas. If [my parents] didn't help me with daycare, I just don't know what I would have done. I used to write on a yellow legal pad that "This is how much my paycheck is going to be. This is the bills. Oh, there's $24 left. Wow." What do you do, go to McDonalds? I think that's what spurs me too, to still be so involved in the community. I know there are some people who need help and sometimes it just takes a little.

Deb: Yes, similarly, I grew up without money, so know

31

what it's like to have no money and have free lunch and those kinds of things. So it was different and sometimes people can't relate to that. I think that even if a person is self-assured and has self-love there is still this self-doubt that can come in. But I find that some people let that self-doubt stop them and others don't. Do you agree? And, do you stop yourself from taking chances and doing things?

Ruth: Well, you know what pushes me? From the time I was young I was always involved in sports. I was a tomboy. I played softball, I played field hockey, and I'm very competitive.
And I think that when I think of "can't" do it, I think that's what makes me say, "Well I should try," because I was just brought up with that competitive mentality. And I'm not competitive to the point that its viciousness, but I do, I want to be better, I want to win, I want to . . .

Deb: Succeed?

Ruth: Yes, succeed.

Deb: And you have now what appears to be a very successful restaurant where you do still give back to the community.

About Her Parents

Deb: What do you think you learned from your parents, from your upbringing, about your self-esteem?

Ruth: My work ethic. Definitely. My father worked harder than anybody I ever knew. He worked for [a trucking company]. He would take the shifts that he could make the most money on. He was an extremely hard worker. He worked swing shift, third shift, whatever. He was a very good mechanic, so he used to work on cars part-time. There was always somebody's car in our garage he was working on.

Deb: For extra money?

Ruth: Right. He worked all the time. And I think that's what made it different, maybe. The difference when I did get divorced and I could have thought, "Well I'm going to sit back, and I'm going to collect welfare or something." The work ethic he instilled in me. To be self-assured, I know I can work. I know no matter what, I can do something, because he did. I saw him do whatever he could do to provide for his family. So I think that helped me.

Deb: So the strong work ethic made you believe that if you worked...

Ruth: Anything was possible. You could really achieve anything. And I was not the best student. I was not the smartest. My brother was good in science and math. Not me; I was more into theater and English.

The Definition

Deb: We talked a little about your journey, your self-doubt, your family. I looked up the definition of self-esteem on Merriam-Webster's online dictionary and I was shocked, and somewhat angry. The first definition, "a confidence and satisfaction in oneself." I agree with that.

Ruth: Yes.

Deb: The second [definition] is simply the words "self-conceit." How do you feel about that?

Ruth: To me, self-esteem is feeling comfortable with yourself. Satisfied with yourself. I think it's simple. So if you do feel comfortable enough to walk into a room you're conceited? Is that what they are trying to say?

Deb: It appears that way. Isn't that terrible?

Ruth: Yes, it is.

Deb: So imagine a thirteen-year-old girl doing a book report on self-esteem, and she finds out one definition of self-esteem is actually self-conceit. So she's conceited if she believes in herself. So what are we teaching?

Ruth: Maybe that's why everybody's perception is so wrong and why we're all so insecure, because maybe we feel like we shouldn't feel successful or comfortable.

Deb: Thinking we're not supposed to feel successful or comfortable. I'm not supposed to walk in and say, "Hey, listen, I'm on this board, or I have a successful business. Or, yes, my practice is doing great." Or whatever, because then I'm conceited. And aren't young girls especially taught that conceit is a horrible thing?

Ruth: They already have such a poor self-image of themselves.

Deb: I don't think any woman in her life wants to be considered conceited.

Ruth: And, to still find that definition in this day and age.

Deb: I know. So, how do you think your self-esteem is

today compared to twenty years ago? Would you say it's improved?

Ruth: I think it's improved because I got past how everybody was thinking about me. I think that was another problem. I was this young divorced mother: What do other people think? Waitressing part-time at night: What do people think? I always worried about what other people thought. And I got past all that. I thought, "Well I have to be happy with myself and know that I provided for my children." I raised them well. I'm very proud of the two of them and it was not easy.

I had a lot of problems with my son. I chose the harder route where I was not everybody's best friend. I was a parent, and if they hated me like they did for two years of their life, they did. But I think that the change came because I worried less about everybody's perception about me. I'm living the way I'm proud of. I'm a good person. I do what I can charity wise. I raised my children well, love my family and my friends are important to me. You learn what is important.

Deb: I think you're right, and I think that's the key to most women as they develop self-esteem. It's not worrying about what other people think. Not that we don't care what other people think, disregarding it entirely.

Ruth: No, but it's not your top priority

Deb: Yes, we shouldn't be worried about, "Oh, did I hurt this person because I didn't let them go first in line at the grocery store?" I mean, it can come down to questioning everything, and then it's, "Do they think I'm a good mother? Do they think I'm a good person? Am I smart enough? Am I pretty enough?" Well, I am enough. I'm absolutely enough. So how did you get there? What allowed you to say, "I'm not going to allow other people's judgments to define me?"

Ruth: Eventually, when I was successful, when I started my business. And my second marriage is a very good, happy, healthy marriage, and my children turned out right. You learn the decisions you made in your life were the right decisions, which gives you—I think—the confidence to say, "I can take chances. I can make good decisions. I'm a smart person." I think seeing your success, and see you're making the right moves is important. Even when I got married to [my current husband], we are married sixteen years, I moved the kids to a new town. I worried was I doing the right thing. I was moving my children to a different school and getting married, and I doubted myself for years. So until you can see that you didn't harm them and that they survived. I think you need to physically see that.

Deb: I agree that with experience it comes.

On Mentoring

Deb: When we put all these other people first and ourselves last, we realize that we're not taking good care, not making the best decision. We're not doing things the best way. But, how do we help younger people get there faster? How do we help your daughter, for example? How do we help her not to have to reach forty before she loves and appreciates herself? What do we do as women and as a community? How do we help?

Ruth: I try to instill in her that she's beautiful and that she's smart. Telling her verbally. Also, I think we need to take some of these women under our wings. Saying, "I'm going to take you here, introduce you to these people," and I think feeling part of something. Maybe mentoring some of these women and saying, "What are your likes and dislikes? I think this organization would be great for you because . . ." Being part of that group working toward a common goal makes you feel better about yourself. So I think that's what we can do with them when they're younger.

Deb: So almost opening them up to experiences that will allow them to succeed, so that they can start to have those successes earlier in life. And have those life experiences that allow them to say, "Oh I'm capable. I can do this, I can run a project, and I can . . ."

Ruth: Exactly, because where else can you go but some place like a Junior League where you are working on a huge fundraising event, a non-profit event. Where you're a project manager. That gives you the experience that I think is invaluable.

Deb: I agree.

Ruth: And I think even other organizations I've been involved in. Just go volunteer, encourage people to just go do something that's going to make them feel better about themselves. That's what I try to do now with my daughter. I drag her to these events. I say, "You're coming with me." I introduce her to everybody. What I try to do is introduce her and expose her to as many people in different situations as possible because I just think that will help her.

Deb: So putting women in positions where they can experience life and meet people. Also I think sometimes women compete with each other. Right?

Ruth: Oh, yes.

Deb: So we have that piece, where instead of being mentors and nurturers of each other, we act as rivals of one another. I don't think it's a huge population—maybe it is. Maybe I just haven't surrounded myself with those people. I don't know, I just think sometimes, women would rather see someone fail than succeed. And I think that comes from our own self-esteem, that we feel that we can't succeed, or we don't care enough about ourselves, so...

Ruth: So there has to be an excuse for it.

Deb: Yes, so it's almost a form of bullying. And we're learning that girls are bullied at least to the same extent as boys and its often passive aggressive, the behind-the-scenes, "Come on, you don't want to be friends with her," type of stuff.

Ruth: I think that's something else that has to change. I make a conscious effort to try to be very supportive of all the women that I meet. If somebody is successful, I'm truly excited. Like, I'm truly excited for your book.

Deb: I know, and I appreciate that.

Ruth: Everybody, even the girls I work with in my business, just starting their careers, I tell them "whatever you need," and I'll give them advice. I'd push some of them who weren't working full time to get into the job market, saying "just try anything." I think we really need to make an effort, if we're going to change this, to really support each other and build each other up. Because if you're just knocking people down, I don't think anything is going to change. That definition's not going to change much.

Deb: Right, one of the reasons for this book is that I

think more people have to start speaking up and telling our stories and experiences. I think people have to know there is a "me" out there. That there are accomplished women who don't/didn't feel it and are sick of it and are going to do something about it. Now I can say, "I do feel good. I grew into it." I wish it didn't take me as long to grow into it and, yes, I still have self-doubt, but I never let it stop me from pursuing something.

Ruth: Why don't you let it stop you?

Deb: I want to succeed. I think it's a competitive thing. I don't know. I think initially I just wanted to see if I could compare to other people. So I wanted to keep doing what I saw other people doing.

Ruth: Right.

Deb: If I saw you achieve something then I might want to achieve it. Not that I wanted to take it away from you, but I wanted to try to achieve it. But as I have gotten older, to recognize I don't have to achieve everything that others achieve and can pick and choose my own goals. So I don't know if I can tell you what drives me. I do know I want to be better. I want to be my best self. When you start to realize all those things we try to strive for. When you get there, you say, "What was the big deal?" So I think really being true to myself drives me. I figured out motivating and inspiring others is what I want to do. Even when I worked at [a previous employer] when I was motivating a team I felt I was in my element. When they put me in sales, with no team to lead, I fell apart. Well, I didn't fall apart, but I just didn't like it. I hated my job; I was depressed. I didn't want to go to work.

So, my mantra then became, motivating and inspiring individuals. You know, I think inside of ourselves we have this piece of us, and we know what our true destiny is. We know what we are supposed to be doing. I think parents will distract us, for fear that it's not profitable. I think partners can distract us. There can be a lot of stumbling blocks, but if we stay true to our authentic selves, and we move in that direction, I think the doors do open up for us. And we can do it.

About Her Husband

Ruth: You know my husband has been my biggest cheerleader. I am so lucky that I don't have somebody who thinks he has to compete with me. I mean, he is so proud of everything I do. You know, that really helps you. You know that I don't like to brag—I'm quiet. You've been out with me. He'll be like, "This is Ruth, and she just did this." But he really has been wonderful. I couldn't ask for better than him.

Deb: It definitely helps if you have a positive partner in your life to help you succeed.

Ruth: I think if you didn't, if you had somebody who felt competitive, it might stop you. You might say, "Well maybe I better not do that." It definitely helps.

Deb: So that is another thing we can do for ourselves. When choosing a partner in life to have someone whose going to support you and who you're going to support. It goes both ways.

Ruth: And I think we have to be cognizant of people who don't have support systems like that, because that's something that we can do to help them. Be there for them.

Deb: Do you have any quote that inspires you?

Ruth: James Dean's "Dream as if you'll live forever. Live as if you'll die today." Just because I believe it. There have been a lot of deaths in my family. There have been a lot of ups and downs. Things change, and we really need to live every day to the fullest. We waste a lot of time. We waste so many days of our lives worrying what people think. "Am I good enough? Am I this...?" You just have to live your life and just trust that things are going to work out, and that quote just reminds me of that. I do try to live that.

Reflections

As with so many women, when her first marriage ended, Ruth thought it was fully her fault, and she looked internally to see what she could have done differently. Over time, and with positive life experiences, her self-esteem and belief in herself became stronger. Ruth embraced her solid work ethic—which was passed on from her father—knowing hard work will bring results. She admits that even though she had self-doubt, she would move forward toward her goals. How does she move ahead even in self-doubt? Ruth credits her participation in team sports, indicating that this helped her gain a competitive spirit that encourages her to try. Regarding the definition of self-esteem, Ruth raises the point that the contradiction in the definition may contribute to the reason we think we "shouldn't feel successful or comfortable." Other factors that contributed to Ruth's self-esteem included becoming less concerned with what other people thought of her and having a good support system. To help young girls and women develop self-esteem, Ruth suggests actively taking some of them under our wings to mentor them. She advocates being a support system for each other, and especially for those who don't have their own positive support systems.

Introspection

*Be who you are and say what you feel, because
those who mind don't matter, and
those who matter don't mind.*
– Bernard M. Baruch

**What do you wish you knew when you were age 20
that might have helped improve your self-esteem (i.e.,
what would you say to your 20 year old self)?**

*I wish I knew how important it was for me to journey
through life without allowing others to hold me back.*
-Tammy G.

*Speak your mind. Don't worry so much about everyone
else.*
-Ruth O.

I would tell myself to stand up for what you want because your opinion does matter!
-Melissa W.

I would tell myself to love and embrace being 20. Learn what you can from your experiences with people, the positive and the negative. Focus on and be thankful for the positive events in your life and on the many good people in this world to admire and learn from.
-Linda C.

I wish I didn't spend so much time worrying about things I couldn't change. I'd probably recommend reading "The Secret" and various positive and motivating books at that younger age. Also, I know I worried about what people thought of me and tried to make others happy. I realized later that I shouldn't put this responsibility on myself. Overall I do not have any regrets and know my journey led me to who I am and where I am today. I feel pretty good about my character and values.
-Janine O.

Find a purpose/move in a direction and get involved in the community and recognize that I had what I needed all along.
-Diane F.

Put your best foot forward and believe in yourself. Go for what you want in life. Appreciate what you have in life and know that you are OK just as you are.
-Joanina L.

I would tell her not to worry so much about things like body image and relationships, which is what I worried about a lot at 20 years old. I would also tell her to spend more time figuring out what makes you happy

because I think those things contribute to self-esteem.
-Christina D.

*No one is perfect. You do not have to subject yourself
to unhealthy relationships just to feel love and feel that
someone cares about you. Respect yourself.*
-Ashely W.

*I feel like my 20-year-old self needs to speak with my
31-year-old self, but I would share that it's important to
use your inner voice to motivate you, not criticize you.
My toughest opponent has always been and continues
to be in the mirror. Learn to look at yourself in a
positive way.*
-Lacey T

*Set your goals a lot higher. Don't just do enough to get
by, push yourself.*
-Ann P.

Mary Jo's Journey

*To uncover your true potential you must first find
your own limits and then you have to have the
courage to blow past them.*
–Picabo Street

I've known Mary Jo (MJ) all of my life. She is a
remarkable person. She is smart and funny, and she is a
great mom. I lost a very dear friend, and MJ was in
town for the funeral. We sat down to this interview
very late in the evening, and we were both exhausted.
Yet, like any good friend, she made time for me.
Growing up I was often jealous of MJ. She seemed to
have it all together, and it wasn't until years later we
were able to be honest with each other about our
insecurities. In that honesty, we were able to help each
other recognize the lack of truth in much of what our
critical voices would say. It was a pleasure to sit with
her in the wee hours of the morning. I am so grateful

to have her in my life.

Deb: So I'm curious about how you learned about self-esteem. How you think you developed it, how you feel about yourself now? What you would like to tell your twenty-year-old self if you could?

MJ: I think self-esteem is something that develops differently in everybody. For me, personally, I didn't have a lot of self-esteem until I was an adult working in my profession. And even when I first started working in my profession I didn't have a lot of self-esteem. I think it was probably because I didn't have people in my life who ever told me good things about myself, which is what I think I needed with my personality, in order to feel like I was smart, or successful.

I never really realized I was smart until I was working in my profession for at least ten years. I knew I was capable because I always got good reviews and things like that, but I remember—and I know it's not like this for everyone—but for me there was a clear turning point. There was a meeting I was in. When I was sitting in this meeting with the Vice President and Controller and about twelve other people, someone raised a complicated legal issue. It was brought up by a nonlegal person. They said, "I've talked to outside counsel about this; it's not the way it's supposed to be done." And the Vice President, who was my current boss at the time said, "How could this happen, I know MJ looked into this two years ago." I said I must have just missed something; maybe I just got it wrong. And he looked at me and said, "No, MJ, you never get anything wrong, so it's not you." So that's really [*smiling*]... He said it in front of everybody. And I thought, "You know, if he could have that much confidence in me, I could have that much confidence in myself."

Deb: That is pretty powerful.

MJ: Yeah, so for me it was pretty clear cut. And I think up until that point some people would say to me, "Oh, how did you work while you were in law school?" And I guess I think, "Yeah, that is kind of amazing." But I never had enough validation to feel like I was anything special. I figured I was just like everybody else and that everything I did was very routine.

Deb: And so, you started to feel smart and...

MJ: Respected.

Deb: And then self-respected?

MJ: Yes, I think so.

Deb: How does it feel then, I guess. Well you said there was a turning point. Does it feel different to have self-esteem versus act it?

MJ: There is. Yes, there's a definite difference, because when I acted like I had self-esteem, I was never always sure of what I was doing. But now that I have it, I know that I'm capable of so much more than I ever thought I was.

Deb: But what about failure?

MJ: Well, I think I'm still going to fail. I'm not perfect. But I'm comfortable with failing now. Like failure doesn't feel the same to me now. Because before I thought, "I'm just this person who really isn't great at anything, but maybe is expected to be," and failure would really hit me hard. But now I can look at it like, well I've had all these successes and I guess I'm bound to fail at some point. And that's okay. Now it just feels fine.

Deb: It almost sounds like acceptance, and feeling fine. Maybe some forgiveness, or self-forgiveness or compassion for self?

MJ: I think probably, I don't know what I would call it. I guess maybe it is forgiveness. It's like a feeling that you don't have to do everything right to be accepted. And to feel like you've been successful.

Deb: Do you feel like being a mother has helped or hurt with you developing a sense of who you are?

MJ: I think that even more so than that "turning point," being a mom—and that turning point came about after I was a mom—but I think that being a mom is something that hasn't shaped me, it hasn't defined me, it *is* me. That's the job I know I do best. That's the job I have never questioned, regardless of whether I thought I was successful in my career. Not because I think I'm a perfect mother, because I don't do everything perfect, but because I feel so comfortable with it. I love it so much that it just feels right, you know? I know that I'm not going to do everything right with my kids. I've made mistakes with them and I'll make mistakes with them again. But of everything I do in my whole life, I know that I get that more right than anything else.

Deb: Well, you supposedly don't get anything wrong in your job.

MJ: Well, according to some people.

Deb: According to some people [*laughing*] so that's

pretty good.

MJ: I just feel that being a mom is obviously the most important job I have.

What Would You Tell Your Younger Self

Deb: Is there something you would want to tell your twenty-year-old self? Something you think you could have said to your twenty-year-old self that would have changed something, or made things happen differently for you?

MJ: Yes. I think that if I were sitting with my twenty-year-old self. And I kind of feel like I have because [my husband's] niece was a lot like I was. I've sat with her and told her, "You could do anything. Don't ever let anybody make you think that you can't because every one of us is capable of being successful. The only one who limits you is yourself." So I think I would have told myself that, and I think it would have made my life a little easier along the way.

Deb: I know. It seems like when you learn so late. . . Well it's never too late and for me, personally, to know now what I didn't know then is great. To really feel it and not just talk the talk. But, yeah, it would have been nice to know then.

MJ: Yeah.

The Definition

Deb: Okay, next thing. I wanted to write a book on self-esteem, so wanted the definition of self-esteem. So I did what everybody would do these days, which is go online to find the definition.

MJ: Right.

Deb: I go to the online dictionary, and one of the definitions is similar to what I think it is, "a sense of self-respect," or something along those lines, which makes perfect sense. Then, the second definition was simply the words "self-conceit." What do you think about that?

MJ: That's funny because I was going to mention that to you. That I think there is a fine line between self-esteem and being too big for your britches, you know? Because I think if you feel like you can do everything right, you never think you're wrong. And that's a bad thing too. So I don't ever want to think I'm the smartest one in the room, and I can never get it wrong. Because then you're never going to grow or learn. That's kind of like thinking that no one can teach you anything, which is ridiculous. So I think it's a fine line you walk. It's really wonderful that [my former boss] told me that, but I also know I do things wrong. You have to know that and not expect too much of yourself, and also not think too much of yourself. I think there's a fine line there though.

Deb: I like your perspective on it. I was actually angry when I read it.

MJ: Really?

Deb: Yes, because self-conceit to me is an exaggeration of oneself, and self-esteem to me is different than self-conceit. Yes, I do believe there is a fine line, but I don't think they're the same thing.

MJ: I agree. I don't think they're the same thing.

Deb: I think you can cross from one to the other, and sometimes we could almost appear to be conceited in some ways and still not be conceited. And I do think it makes it hard for women to share our own successes. We're not supposed to make anyone else feel bad. So to talk about how I might have accomplished this, or I might have gotten promoted. Is that self-esteem or is that self-conceit?

MJ: I don't know because I'm just thinking back to tonight when I was talking about my kids. And I have a lot of self-esteem when it comes to being a mother. But when I talk about my kids sometimes I think I sound really conceited because I'm bragging about them so I think that I still don't think self-esteem and self-conceit are the same thing. I mean, I think that people can often perceive that they're the same thing. When a woman shows her self-esteem, she just seems like she's kind of cocky, versus a man showing the same just looks normal. You know, powerful.

Deb: I know.

MJ: But I think that you can. It doesn't matter what other people think. It matters what you think of yourself, and so I just really think you need to make sure that you always know you're fallible, because everybody is. And that's okay. That's the thing. I think some women get really upset when they have a failure in their lives. We all do. I mean I think everybody would. But I think knowing that that's okay is so important. You can still have self-esteem and not do everything right.

Deb: Yes. You had said that it seems to be cockiness when a woman talks about certain things. Should it be, or should we be changing how we allow women and accept women self-validating? Because we don't always get validation from other places, but then are not allowed to validate ourselves by talking about our successes. It almost seems there is this social inequality here, right?

Socially it's not acceptable: A woman should be quiet and reserved about her successes. She should just keep them to herself so that she's not being conceited. But, what about being proud? Can't you just be proud that you're a good mother? Can't you just be proud of your children? And what message are we sending to the nieces—to the thirteen-year-olds? So a thirteen-year-old going out and finding the definition [of self-esteem] that says "self-conceit." What are we saying to her?

MJ: Well, I think this is really complicated because I think that we as women want to be treated the same as men and do the same things men do and not be treated differently for it. But I actually think it's the opposite. I think men should be acting more the way women act. Either extreme, not validating or over-validating, is wrong. I just think there is more of a middle ground of where we are and where men are. That being said, of course, we should be proud of the things we do, and we shouldn't be ashamed about speaking about them, or having them written somewhere, or being acknowledged in some way.

Deb: Yeah, I don't know that all men sit around and tout their successes either.

MJ: No, not the real strong and powerful men. I think the more times you see [over-validating], you see the people who really don't have self-esteem doing that.

Deb: So it seems there is a difference between

confidence and conceit, self-esteem or self-conceit. It is
complicated. It's a feeling that I know that I didn't
always have that allows me to feel empowered. Not
powerful or power over others, but empowered. I know
it's different. I just don't know how to talk about it and
to let women know that it's okay to have this feeling.

MJ: It's not an easy feeling to describe. And it's not
necessarily going to feel the same to everybody.

Deb: You're right, it's not. As a matter of fact, when I
talk with [another woman featured in the book], she
said "I just never felt that. I just never considered myself
to not do what I wanted to do," and she's the least
conceited person I know.

MJ: You want people to be able to walk around with
confidence, with that level of confidence, without being
seen to be conceited.

Deb: I don't want people to just look confident.

MJ: But to feel it.

Deb: Yes, to feel and truly believe it. Confidence—like
you said—is that, "I know I may fail, but I also know
I'm capable."

MJ: It's a shame that so many women don't feel that
way. And when you think of us not feeling that way
when you know we're reasonably bright, reasonably
attractive, educated, and yet we can feel this lack of
confidence. So then the people you really need to help
are those young girls who haven't recognized even that
yet. Everybody's capable of something.

Deb: Absolutely, capable of something. Not everything.

That's too much pressure.

MJ: No, but everyone is capable of being successful in their own way. You know what you should do with this?

Deb: What?

MJ: You should talk to some teenage girls. You really should.

Deb: I know. I hope this is a start of a bigger conversation. We've got to start asking how we can help each other. I know I have an ego, and I know sometimes I can come off as conceited, but I have never in my life felt conceited. I barely felt worthy to be in the same room with some women. And that's a sin, because I'm a decent woman.

MJ: Right, you're just as worthy.

Deb: I'm just as worthy as anyone to sit in that room, and to think that nobody would want to talk with me or I have nothing to offer is terrible. It's a terrible feeling. I do think this is the start. Let's talk to some women. Ask, "Did you have self-esteem? How did you develop it? Did your mother have it? What was her upbringing?" If you think of the generation who raised us, women were still fighting for rights to be in the workplace, let alone making the same money as men. So why would we expect they would have the tools to give us positive self-esteem? No one was passing it on to them. And that's okay if every mother can't give that to their daughter, but somebody's got to give it to young women. Somebody's got to let them know that it exists. Sometimes it's that one person, that one teacher or coach who can make an impact, and you don't have to wait until you're forty years old. We need to be mentors to women and to all of those young teens so that they can grow up to be empowered. Not overpowering, but empowered.

Impact on Young Men

MJ: And I'll tell you what, Debbie, this goes even further. You talk about women and teenage girls. Teenage boys have so much less self-esteem than you would ever think. And the expectation for them is so much higher, and it shouldn't be and that's the flip side that I see. The pressure on boys to be the "man" and to be so much more successful, that much quicker, and to achieve certain things as teenagers.

Deb: When you talk about [your oldest son], the things I hear you say he's doing, and think, "Can't he just relax?"

MJ: And it's certainly not pressure I'm putting on him. Not pressure [my husband] is putting on him. We want him to do things he wants to do. Its pressure society puts on him because he sees what everyone else is doing and thinks he needs to do the same things to be accepted. "I can't *not* take that honors class because then kids are going to look at me like I'm stupid. And the one thing I have going for me is that I'm a smart kid, and I'm a smart athlete. There aren't that many smart athletes." And try telling him otherwise, Deb.

Deb: I don't think you can just tell teenagers anything, and as a parent all you can do is lay the foundation. There seems to be a lot of pressure on boys and then men to work seven days a week to provide for the family. To work for that big house to never have time to be in it. I'm not sure young men, or anyone for that matter wants to work to that excess, but it's the pressure that society puts on them. And the society is us; we're the society.

MJ: It's not just teens. It's young kids too. It's older people too.

Deb: Well look at the bullying going on. Why do we have to bully? Well, we bully when we don't feel good about ourselves. So that means fewer people are feeling good about themselves.

MJ: It's terrible when a six-year-old comes home and says. "My dad doesn't have [what your dad has]." Who cares? But somehow they learn to care, and it's all a form of bullying. Who should even know that at age six? Why are people telling you that? All you should know is you have a dad, and he's home at night.

Deb: And he's a good guy, treats you good, and plays ball with you. We need a shift in society. We start with each of us one at a time and then shift the paradigm. The focus now is on women and girls, but I want to then start the conversation with men and boys. I see men in my practice, and they can feel like crap and have low self-esteem.

MJ: It's so hard. There are so many different factors leading into it, and women need to know that women are part of the problem too. Some successful women are part of the problem. We're all part of the problem. Working moms don't respect stay-at-home moms, and stay-at-home moms don't respect working moms. You know, we all need to fit together. We can all work together; we can all be valued. It's important for us to have working women. It's important for us to have stay-at-home moms. It's important for us to have men who stay at home with their kids. Just like it's important for us to have blue collar workers and white collar workers. I mean, it's all important. There's just no synergy. The expectations are very high these days. It's just very difficult to establish that self-esteem.

Deb: And there are all these material things that we try to put on us too to try to make us feel better about ourselves, and you know we're not feeling it inside. Maybe with these conversations we can help people begin to feel better about themselves. Thanks for sitting with me.

Reflections

For MJ there was an "aha" moment later in her life that shifted her perception of herself. In that moment, she came to a realization she was capable of doing almost anything. She admits improved self-esteem allows her to be more comfortable with failing, and she doesn't feel so much pressure to do everything right. She accepts that we will all fail sometimes, but we will also succeed some of the time. MJ also makes a good point that self-esteem can not only develop differently for different people, but may also feel different to each person. In addition, finding balance between acceptable behaviors in men versus women may be helpful to the process; allowing similar behaviors from women to be seen as powerful, instead of cocky. MJ also points out the challenges facing boys in our culture and the impact to their self-esteem and that low self-esteem is no longer just an issue impacting girls and women. MJ reminds us it is important to accept each other and that it's essential for our society to have a variety of women with a variety of talents, and for us to support each other in the roles we choose.

Introspection

"My Dad's quote isn't famous, but it should be: 'Never cut yourself down...there are plenty of people in the world who will do it for you.'"
-Ann P.

Did you ever act as if you had self-esteem when you didn't feel it?

Growing up was difficult for me. My father was in the Marine Corps so we moved a lot. I met a lot of people over the years but it wasn't easy getting and keeping friends. On the outside I adapted well and seemed approachable, but inside I was battling feelings of not fitting in.
-Tammy G.

I do a lot of acting when I don't feel it, but am getting better.
-Ruth O.

Yes, I have held various leadership positions. I have confidence and feel good about myself when I am working and knowledgeable about the material.
-Melissa W.

I have worked in the business field since I was 17 years old. At times it was overwhelming for me and sometimes I felt intimidated by older coworkers. As I learned my new responsibilities and tackled the "hurdles," I became more confident in my abilities which in turn helped to improve my self-esteem.
-Linda C.

During elementary school and early high school years I did not have the best self-esteem. I consider myself somewhat of an introvert, so these feelings were rarely shared with others. To others it might have appeared as though I was confident and self-assured, but inside, not so much. There were times when I encountered nasty and mean people growing up. Unfortunately there are many unkind individuals in the world that try to bring you down. Some can be very hurtful. So you have to dig down deep and reassure yourself that their words have no relevance and don't deserve any of your time or energy.
-Janine O.

I would like to have been born with great self-esteem, but that is normally not the case. My self-esteem has been developed through self-discovery, and I am truly happy with who I am and have become as an individual. Looking back, it would have been nice to be on top of my game when I was 20. Maybe I wouldn't have spent as much time in bars or looking for a boyfriend/husband that somehow I believed I needed to complete myself. There have been times when I have been unsure of a move (public speaking, career

changes) but I find that if I 'pretend' —no one knows that I might be doubting myself. After I get to the other side, it actually improves my self-confidence when I can look back at what I had accomplished (of course fooling everyone that I had no idea if I could accomplish what I set out to do). No one will know that you doubt yourself unless you tell them. It allows you to push yourself a little harder to see what you can do.
-Diane F.

Often....always trying to appear confident in the work place, as well as, in social situations, etc.
-Joanina L.

Though not any specific one time, but in general, when I am around men at work who are in higher level or more powerful positions, I act as though I have a higher self-esteem than I really do. Some make me feel as though I should have a low self-esteem and some of it is what I project onto myself.
-Christina D.

I did when I was a teenager. I was a cheerleader so everyone thought I felt great about myself, little did they know I judged myself every day. I would laugh and put a smile on my face to pretend I was okay. As an adult, I sometimes will mask low self-esteem with being successful. Most don't know that I sometimes have low self-esteem because professionally I do so well.
-Ashely W.

Absolutely! As a part time position I instruct aerobic classes. On a weekly basis I'm expected to demonstrate power, strength and provide motivational cues for members. Quite often, (especially after having my first child) I was very self-critical and lacking self-esteem; but I disguised it.
-Lacey T

When I was a young student teacher I did a lot of "acting" to make it look like I was smarter and braver than I actually was. My self-esteem was not great, but I knew the students would "smell" fear so I pretended for 12 weeks. By the end of the twelve weeks I actually became very confident.
-Ann P.

Laura's Journey

Change your thoughts and you change your world.
-Norman Vincent Peale

Laura has a natural calming effect on those around her. It's interesting because she doesn't view herself that way but that's how she appears and it is what makes her easy to talk to. Laura is funny, likes to laugh and doesn't take herself too seriously. Maybe this is because—as a therapist—she understands life can be very serious, so you need to be able to laugh and keep your sense of humor. Laura is also very smart in an unassuming way, and this modesty is something I appreciate in her. She has many talents including being a great mom, making the best birthday cakes for any one of her three children and practicing Reiki when time allows. Our friendship continues to grow, and I am thankful she has become part of my life.

Deb: I want to learn about you and your self-esteem. Do you have and did you always have self-esteem?

Laura: No, that's the easy answer to that. Or I haven't always had it. Where I am now, I think being a therapist for the last umpteen years has very much cultivated my awareness of my own issues. And I don't know if it's self-esteem in a traditional definition, but for me relationship issues sometimes bring up thoughts of being unworthy. These feelings come up for me always. But at this point because of my awareness, when negative feelings start to rise I kind of recognize they are not accurate feelings for what is going on. Not an accurate perception for what's going on, and so I can recognize it and say that something is going on for me, or that I'm vulnerable, tired or sick, sad or whatever. That kind of cracks that door to the places where I still feel vulnerable.

Deb: So do you think that you have to be a therapist in order to figure out, or develop, positive self-esteem?

Laura: No, no. Not at all. I think that for me personally, this process would have taken much longer if I wasn't a therapist. I started being a therapist right away. I went to school straight through because I didn't know what else I was going to do. I didn't want to get a job and thought I might as well go to grad school. I always thought about being a therapist, and to be a therapist you need to go to grad school, so why not? So I was doing that in my early twenties when I was just becoming an adult and just realizing all of that stuff and all my family issues were in full bloom at that point and all my personal issues were in full bloom at that point. And my natural tendencies personality wise, genetically, culturally, are to be quiet, to pull back, to distance, dissociate from feeling, to say, "Let's not talk about it. Let's avoid it. Let's pretend it doesn't happen." But becoming a therapist, and being mindful that I wanted to be a decent one, meant that I couldn't avoid that for any real length of time, or any depth. I could do it occasionally and move in and out of it somewhat, but not on a very real level. Being a therapist very much kept me in touch with my feelings, and my process, and what I was dealing with, and so I think that I may have eventually gotten to the point where I'm at now, but I don't think I would be here at this age [thirty-five].

Deb: And so, what I'm hearing—and it's something that's becoming a theme I've been hearing as I'm talking with people—is that "I feel better about myself now, but those things still do come up and I need to challenge them and make sure I know that it's not a reasonable thought." It's not reasonable to think, "I'm not worthy," or people don't like me or whatever the thoughts are that we carry with us.

Laura: And I have some expectation that those [thoughts] will be there always, and that's my shadow work, my vulnerabilities. I don't know. It sort of feels like a horror movie. If I hadn't done this, I wonder what kind of relationships I would have ended up in, what kind of friendships I would have cultivated, and what that would have meant for my health and wellbeing too.

Deb: Yes, and I think that you've done a good job in your work too, and one of the reasons I wanted to talk with you is that you inspire me by your presence—by who you are. Although you tell me about some of the anxiety and nervousness you have, you always appear to be just calm. And I get that's just part of the therapist thing, but I think it's also part of your nature to calm people. You have this quiet confidence that I'm not sure you know you exude. Just a subtlety in your presence that makes me feel like, "Oh, this is someone I could emulate in this behavior."

Laura: It doesn't feel that way in my experience of it, but thank you.

Deb: You're welcome. And I think we don't tell people and talk with people truly about how we feel about them. I think people really need to hear the good stuff as much as they hear the bad stuff. We don't know the impact it might have on people, but where we can tell them the good things we should.

Laura: And this is one of the places where I feel really lucky, and I admit this is going to feel kind of weird to keep talking about myself, but I'm supposed to be doing that.

Deb: Yes, you're supposed to be.

Laura: So, I feel really lucky because of my mom and the fact that she does tell me not only how she feels about me, but she has also shared her journey with me, and because of the other friends that I have—particularly in that circle—that are, they're psychologically minded. They're spiritual people. They're aware. I mean these are people who have women's groups and see spiritual directors. You know? And so have allowed me to be with them in that and they're all very expressive and very nice people an don't hesitate to and even if it's just "I like being with you, this is nice"

Deb: Just very expressive in sharing love. So if we could surround ourselves with people like that I think that's important too.

Laura: Well it makes it a little easier to, you know, ultimately, and I hesitate to say this because I don't know how much I feel it, but I want to feel it. And what

I convey to the people I work with is that ultimately it has to come from us, that grounded sense underneath it all that "I'm really okay, so we can hear what other people are saying, and feel what other people are saying." But that external validation is really nice.

Deb: Yes, yes. And you're right: The internal piece is the piece of you that says, "I'm not going to listen to that [negative thought] because that voice isn't healthy for me, and it's not true. It's basically lying to me, and I don't feel good when I hear it, so why should I listen to that voice?" I mean, we should have a voice of reason, but it doesn't have to be self-degrading. That's the voice that we often hit ourselves over the head with and make ourselves feel bad about things that don't apply.

Laura: And that's where it comes up most for me. Some of it fits with my social [anxiety]. I don't really like going out. It's a confidence thing for me. The job that I had [in college] was public speaking and social interaction. I initially went there because I liked history, and they let me work at the library.

Deb: Where you were alone?

Laura: I was. I was alone. They gave me letters, soldiers' letters, and wanted me to type them into the computer database, which was really neat. But then I got there and was getting comfortable and someone said, "Well, why don't you work here this summer?" I said sure, and that was a huge accomplishment. I can identify that as being a big catalyst for me having to practice small talk and seeing that I could do it. I could say something stupid, and it didn't matter. But I realized the majority of the time, I was able speak without saying something "stupid."

Deb: I think sometimes our self-esteem or self-doubt will get in the way of us trying things. And to force ourselves to do those things, even when we might have some doubt.

Laura: I'm not sure I would have just gone and worked there if I didn't know some of the layout, and some of the workers seemed to like me. They were encouraging me to do it.

Deb: But you still did it. You still had to make that choice inside to say, "I'm going to be okay. Let's do it," and to learn how to breathe.

Laura: Right. But I just feel really lucky in having some support in that. I think if it was just me in the world, I'd be a hermit. [*Sarcastically*] Never anxious at all.

About Her Mother

Laura: My mom and I carry some similar vulnerable places, but had different childhoods. Very different childhoods. She was the oldest of six, and her parents were very young when they had her. They were only nineteen or twenty when she was born and admitted to her later, "We made a lot of mistakes" with her. They were very hard on her. She would come home with a 98 percent on a test but would be asked, "Where are the other two points?" And she was valedictorian of her class.

Deb: Wow.

Laura: But she was the oldest of six, taking care of younger siblings at the age of two. So she had a lot of expectations, and she felt she needed to be perfect. And I carry that too, but I did not get that from them, so I don't know where that comes from other than it being sort of passed down.

Deb: That's one of my philosophies, and I think we were just talking about it. Family secrets and family histories, how we carry things. I think in just the way our mothers or fathers carry things, we can start to carry things. So it might not have been what your mother said, but the way she acted—always being responsible, always doing the right thing, always being there for people—that you might have learned.

Laura: Right. I might have learned some of that there. It's interesting because a couple friends of mine and I have talked about it too as being the "good sibling." Ending up, for a number of reasons, like the good kid. The one that—because the other siblings require energy, or are getting in trouble, or aren't doing well, or whatever—doesn't get in trouble.

Deb: Which might not be fair, but we can't change that.

Laura: Right. So I'm not sure I would do it differently. I don't think I'd go back and say, "I'm going to do some stuff. I still feel the same way." I still wouldn't want my parents to go through anything they didn't have to. I still prided myself on getting good grades anyway and that's part of me so I don't know if I would have done anything differently.

Deb: Well, I do think it's a journey. One of the things I want to talk with you about is the definition for self-esteem and thirteen-year-old girls and what we could do as an older generation.

Laura: This is good because I have daughters. I know they have to go through it, and I can't just implant it before they hit [their teenage years].

Deb: Yeah, the critical voices they hear in middle school and now it's starting earlier, even in third and fourth grade.

The Definition

Deb: I looked up online in the Merriam-Webster dictionary. I looked a couple places and the dictionary had two definitions. The first definition was something we pretty much understand and it was a healthy belief in oneself, healthy self-respect. But the second definition was two words and those two words were "self-conceit."

Laura: Really?

Deb: Yes, really. So what do you think about self-esteem being defined as self-conceit?

Laura: I don't think I would put that in the definition of self-esteem because I generally view self-esteem as the positive side of the coin. But if we're using self-esteem defining it as the whole coin, then I guess self-conceit would be the shadow side or the other side of the coin as you know narcissism, or conceit.

Deb: Yes, self-conceit is an overly inflated feeling of oneself. An inflated view of oneself.

Laura: That would be the other end of that spectrum, or negative self-esteem. Although generally when I think of positive self-esteem I don't think of it going to that end, as it being on that end.

Deb: You don't think of it as self-conceit, right?

Laura: Right. But I guess the bell curve that's self-esteem of positive in the middle, low on one side and I guess higher would be...

Deb: But they didn't write "self-degradation," right? That would be an opposite or another side too.

Laura: Right. I don't know. I don't think I ever heard of anybody saying self-esteem being self-conceit.

Deb: And the other end of that, as I'm looking this definition up and as young individuals, you know, imagine a thirteen-year-old girl online doing a little report on self-esteem and she finds this definition. What teenager wants to be considered conceited?

Laura: None.

Deb: So now we are teaching our children that self-esteem is a bad thing, because to be conceited isn't a good thing.

Laura: I've actually, worked with people through their hesitation in finding change and moving their perspective in talking about themselves. There seems to be a fear that, "If I stop holding on to this [perspective], then I'm going to become one of those jerks." And that fear of moving to that other end of the spectrum. Thinking that it's better to be walked on and be considered a nice person than it is to stand up for myself and be considered conceited.

Deb: How many times are we told, "Don't brag. It's not nice to brag about yourself."

Laura: In particular with women, and this has hopefully gotten somewhat better, but is still true in my generation, "Don't hurt people's feelings." "Be nice to people." I remember in high school and in college, not having that more-centered sense of self and being concerned that saying "no" meant I was being mean. Not wanting to hurt somebody's feelings.

Deb: Well, because women are socialized differently than men. Men are socialized to be in pacts, and there's usually a leader of the pact and guys just could fight and get over it. And women usually don't express negative emotion. You're not supposed to hurt people's feelings so we almost go to the other side. Instead of expressing hurt, saying "Hey, you know you hurt my feelings when you did that." Instead, we hold onto it and make ourselves feel even worse and then also feel angry with people for something they don't even know about.

Laura: Right it's not processed—not dealt with or talked about—so it doesn't go anywhere.

Deb: But as the "good girl," you're not supposed to say anything. You shouldn't confront anyone.

Laura: You should take care of people. You should be nice to people, do what they ask you to do. That can lead to some pretty scary dynamics when your self-esteem is low.

Deb: It's ugly, this whole self-esteem thing, this self-conceit. If we [women] could recognize our accomplishments wouldn't that improve our self-esteem? And "accomplished" doesn't have to mean you earned a million degrees or that you have X dollars of money. It means you're a really good mother, or you're a really good friend—those things that aren't material. A friend said that sometimes stay-at-home moms are treated differently even by working moms. Where is the respect of each other in order for us to learn self-respect?

On Judgment

Laura: Well because of where I'm at in my life, most of my friends are in significant relationships and having kids. Some women staying home and other women having to work, and you have economic struggles. I've had a lot of friends posting stuff on social media and basically making judgment. Why aren't we as women supporting each other in recognizing a lot of stuff has to happen for economic reasons? There may be different environments and different support systems and all sorts of stuff, but the judgment even between women is so huge. Like breastfeeding and not breastfeeding, and making your own baby food and not making your own baby food, and do we use disposable diapers? It just never ends. It would be nice to just support each other in the honesty in the struggle.

Deb: And in the acceptance of being different from one another. It's really okay, and it doesn't make me better or worse than you. It just makes me "me" and you "you." And there's nothing wrong with that. I'm going to be the best me that I can be, and you should be the best you that you can be. And then together we should be helping each other, lifting each other up.

Laura: Where do you think that judgment piece comes from? Because I hate to stereotype that women are more judgmental. I don't know if we're more verbal in our judgment, or because we are more relational, are we more aware of all these things?

Deb: Well I think we not only judge others, but we also

judge ourselves very harshly.

Laura: I don't know if I know any mother who considers herself a good mom.

Deb: I know someone who can finally say it, that she feels confident that she is a good mom. She said "I'm not perfect, and there is a difference." And there *is* a difference. It seems we tend to think in order to be good at something, to be an excellent mother; you have to be a "perfect" mother. And that's not possible. So, I think, again, it goes to perfection. Judgment I think is a defense mechanism. I don't think everybody judges, but I do think we self-judge, and that sometimes we do talk about other people to kind of deflect it from ourselves for a little while.

Laura: What do you think is harder: Not being judgmental of other people or not being judgmental of yourself?

Deb: I think not being judgmental of yourself is harder.

Laura: I agree, and in a lot of different contexts. Having a woman come into my office and say she was sexually assaulted and not being able to name it as such and blaming herself. "If I wasn't drinking, if I wasn't wearing that particular outfit, if I didn't make out with him for fifteen minutes before. . . ." And to that same person I ask them, "If your friend came and talked to you and said this happened, what would you tell your friend? What would you call it for her? Would you blame her? What would you say to her?" And almost always they say, "It's not your fault." But for them that is not the immediate response at all. It's as if that self-esteem piece doesn't allow us to consider ourselves to be as worthy as everybody else.

Deb: It's easier to forgive others. We are so forgiving of others. We allow people to make mistakes all the time. I think we should have a day where we don't judge anyone. We don't judge self or others. We try it for one day, to not talk negatively about any person, especially ourselves.

As a Mom

Deb: What about family influence? I think parents play a role even if subtle. You said, "How can I instill [self-esteem] in my daughters? I wish I could just implant it right in the middle of their hearts."

Laura: That's stuff we talk about now. I have a nine-year-old son too. I'm having conversations with him and my husband and saying, "Just because you say, 'Give me a kiss,' doesn't mean she has to." If they say "no," for whatever reason—they're tired, busy doing something else—they don't have to. But then the boys do the "boo boo lip" and say, "Ah, come on." I tell them, "No, don't do that."

Deb: Yes, she said "no."

Laura: She said "no." No is no, and you have respect that. I remember saying something to my husband and he's said, "But I'm 'daddy.'" But what do you want her to learn when she goes to college? If some boy gives her "boo boo lip" and says, "But, I love you," how do you want her to respond? And it was like a light bulb went off. He said, "Well I don't want her doing. . . ." And I said, "Then this is where we start. We start with you. You being her father and giving her permission to say 'yes' and say 'no.'" And for my son, to learn no means no. If your sister doesn't want you to touch her, then

DEB PAVLICO MS, LPC

she doesn't want you to touch her. And the same holds true for you. If you don't want her to touch you right then or you don't want to play right now, you have the right to set limits and boundaries and say no and then have that respected.

What Would You Tell Young Women?

Deb: What would you like to tell the twenty-year-olds right now, or that thirteen-year-old? How do we start to change this?

Laura: "You're beautiful. You're beautiful." You know? And a bigger sense of what that is and not the sexualized "beautiful." Having people be loved in a non-egocentric, non-sexualized way which is what you think of as parent-child or familial love that a lot of people don't get.

Deb: Yes, and even if we're not related, I think we have to—as teachers, as professors, as professionals, as coworkers—to point out the good in people. You know, there's a philosophy, "Catch your kids doing something right." Can we catch each other doing things right and point it out? Also, to allow kids [and others] to make mistakes, and give some positive feedback so they can come out of it feeling positive. Knowing that it's just a mistake, everyone makes them and you don't have to beat yourself up over it.

Laura: Start fostering self-esteem.

Deb: Yes, to start fostering it, exactly. There are these amazing, amazing individuals who just don't think they're amazing.

Laura: That's something I've come across in women.

Some of them have a sense that you have to be perfect to be worthy. So to be a good mom, you have to be perfect, which isn't possible. To be a good mom you're going to make a lot of mistakes. In order to be a good friend, employee, and partner you're going to make mistakes. There is this perfectionism that no one could possibly live up to.

Deb: If you're going to wait for you to be perfect, then you're never going to live. You're never going to get meaning out of having the children, the relationship, or the career. If you're waiting to be "perfect," you'll be waiting a lifetime.

Reflections

Laura said she developed self-esteem in her twenties, as part of her self-exploration as a therapist. She admits self-doubt still comes up for her, but she recognizes and challenges it more easily than when she was younger. She believes self-doubt presents itself to many of us regularly. The factors contributing to her journey include a supportive mother and nurturing mentors who provided positive feedback when she was younger. To fend off lack of confidence, she has put herself in situations that help build that confidence. Laura also discusses women being socialized to please others and admits we may ask ourselves if saying "no" means we are hurting people's feelings, without recognizing we have a right to our own feelings. We discussed women's roles in judging each other, and she admits believing we are harder on ourselves than on others, recognizing that judging isn't helpful to women overall. She looks to a time when we can support each other in the "honesty in the struggle."

Most poignant for me was Laura's example of educating the men (fathers and sons) in her life to understand they are powerful teachers of her daughters. It's important that fathers and mothers give children permission to say no, to have a voice and an opinion. Maybe not always agreeing with those opinions, but respecting them.

Introspection

The worst loneliness is to not be comfortable with yourself.
– Mark Twain

How did you develop or improve your self-esteem? Was there an "aha" moment, or a subtle shift. Can you briefly explain your experience?

I began to spend more time outdoors. I did a lot of hiking, biking, and meditation by myself. The alone time allowed me to tap into who I truly was as a person. Being out in nature gave me a sense of belonging. I felt very safe and empowered.
-Tammy G.

Going through life's experiences teaches you to be strong.
-Ruth O.

I think I always had lower self-esteem—not a great deal of confidence. When I was younger I had more

confidence because I didn't know any better. My self-esteem has gotten worse with age because I suffer with self-image issues—it is hard to age.
-Melissa W.

My self-esteem has improved as I've matured. Over the years I have gone through so many life experiences and from each experience I have grown more confident. I have learned that in addition to taking care of others you also need to practice self-care and put yourself first sometimes.
- Linda C.

I was very fortunate growing up to have parents that always encouraged me to follow my dreams. My Mom especially would verbally compliment me on my talents, whether studying hard for an exam and getting good grades or playing sports in grade school and high school. Her encouragement and faith in me helped me achieve many, if not all, of my accomplishments. My Dad was more quiet and a man of few words, but I knew he was always very supportive and proud of me. I think there was a gradual, subtle growth in my development of self-esteem. I always had to work hard for good grades. I chose to set high goals to maintain honors and a high GPA. I never wanted to settle for being an 'average' student. As time went by I started to see good results from applying myself. Overall I feel this helped to build my confidence and elevated my feelings of self-worth.
-Janine O.

When I was in my twenties, I remember feeling frustrated that I couldn't seem to work myself into an actual career, and that I somehow lacked what I needed to succeed. I was continually comparing myself to people who had seemed to have it "all together". I felt

so unfocused and like I was floundering without a direction. After some time with a therapist, I remember saying that a particular person "had it together". In that discussion, the therapist helped me find that I was really no different than the people I perceived to have this "togetherness". I had it all of the time and that I already had what I needed to succeed. Big "Aha" moment for me. Another "Aha" moment was when I was trying to figure what to do with my life and the direction I wanted to go (still don't know LOL). Realizing that I just needed to set myself on a path or to begin just moving in "some" direction—it didn't have to be the "perfect'" direction.
-Diane F.

I believe we have several small and large moments that are life changing....mine changed considerably when I got divorced and for the first time in my life was on my own. I had a lot to prove to myself. However, I believe as for self-esteem a significant "aha" moment happened when I received my first promotion at work. That reality considerably altered me and how I viewed myself.
-Joanina L.

I developed it initially through observing adults, mostly women, when I was younger and continue to work on it today. I do this through challenging myself, learning from mistakes and keeping an open and positive mind. For me, it's been more of a subtle shift because I continue to grow as a person, which improves my self-esteem. Not to say that there weren't a few "aha" moments along the way, in which I surprised even myself at my response to certain events (i.e., parent's divorce, bad relationships, career choice). I also try to remain true to the things I believe in.
Christina D.

My father played a big part in my self-esteem. The first thing was very annoying, at the time. Whenever I needed information (in the days before the internet) like store hours or information on certain items in a store, or even checking on a relative in the hospital, he would always make me call, from about eleven years old, instead of him doing it for me. I HATED it, but it somehow gave me confidence. The second thing my Dad would do was, even when I was a very young girl, whenever I said anything negative about myself (i.e., "I'm stupid," "I'm short") he would say "Never cut yourself down...there are plenty of people in the world who will do it for you."
-Ann P.

There are still some days that I struggle, but not as much as I used to. I improve it by focusing on the good. Remembering that I deserve to be loved and I am a good person. I find comfort in daily positive quotes and make sure I read at least five per day.
-Ashely W.

During my academic path at secondary school. Initially I attended a community college to develop better academic strategies, upon successful completion I enrolled with a University. The two year challenge was a constant reminder of how I was in control; I was much more prepared than I was telling myself. After taking some time off to work, I re-entered schooling at the graduate level. This practical experience assisted me in feeling good about my decisions and my abilities. Attending college on multiple levels, academically performing, being mentally stimulated, and applying my knowledge assisted in gaining confidence and increased self-esteem.
-Lacey T.

Natasha's Journey

Believe you can and you're halfway there.
-Theodore Roosevelt

I have known Natasha for a few years. When I met her, she was a student and I was a staff member. It's typical for some students to be quiet around staff, but even as I got to know her, she was still quiet. What I learned is she is not necessarily quiet, but thoughtful in her words. Unlike me, who can talk for the sake of talking, Natasha seems to talk only when she has something to say. It's a characteristic I value and appreciate. She is smart, and her quietness can be disarming for some, as they might wonder what she's thinking. This quiet presence gives the appearance that Natasha is very comfortable in her own skin. I learned that she is still growing in her journey, but like so many women, is further along then I think she even realizes. I am glad to know her.

Deb: I know you grew up in a situation that wasn't perfect. I just find that you're confident now and are a role model for people. I don't know if you see yourself as that.

Natasha: No.

Deb: When I see you, I see a person who seems so comfortable that it almost makes me uncomfortable, at times that I'm not as comfortable. Those old self-worth thoughts come up for me sometimes. So where are you with your "Am I worthy" or self-esteem today?

Natasha: I think it is a constant struggle. I turned thirty last year. I now have to think about my age. I just think how it is a constant struggle, that I want to embrace my age and when things start coming up like grey hair, and the fact it takes longer to look a certain way. Or when you exercise, it's not just that you do some jumping jacks, and you're in super shape. Now it takes a lot more effort. How can I embrace my age when it continues in a world that doesn't embrace age? I want to be the person who lets myself go grey and accepts my wrinkles as just wisdom.

Deb: Yes, we should be able to appreciate that, but the media doesn't appreciate that. And then society says we don't appreciate that, and then young girls learn that they can only be appreciated if they look or dress a certain way. So it can be a struggle. Do you remember how your self-esteem developed? Do you remember how you felt as a kid?

Natasha: I remember having very low self-esteem. I've always had brains and knew how to use them. And I think that was always a source of resilience and hope for me, but I remember always feeling shame over my appearance, how I compared to peers, feeling that I lacked the social skills, not knowing how to interact with people. Sometimes I felt embarrassed about my intelligence.

Deb: Because?

Natasha: I remember being teased about it. One memory that sticks in my head was in seventh grade graduation, before we went into high school. I won a lot of awards and people were teasing me. As I was getting up for the fifth or sixth time, rather than feeling proud, I felt shame in some way.

Deb: Self-conscious?

Natasha: Very self-conscious of every step I was taking.

Deb: As if, you had outperformed other people, and that was bad of you. How sad is it that a young girl will feel that? So how did that change then? You knew you were proud of your smarts, knew you had them. How did you deal with your smarts as you entered high school?

Natasha: I focused. I was so driven about education; I poured myself into writing, journaling, music. I found myself having very close relationships with my teachers, maybe even at the expense of peer relationships. And they were very encouraging of me, and I think that was a source of comfort.

The Definition

Deb: I was looking up definitions of self-esteem online. How would you define self-esteem?

Natasha: I define self-esteem as a balance of worthiness and confidence that you need to feel worthy as a person and as a human being. So you have to have the talent to carry out what's important to you.

Deb: So a balance in competence. What if I told you I found two definitions for self-esteem. The one was positive; the other was "self-conceit."

Natasha: Self-conceit?

Deb: Yes, to be conceited, to have an exaggerated opinion of one's own self-worth.

Natasha: That I don't have.

Deb: What if you're thirteen and see this and find out to feel good about yourself you have to be conceited, and I'm wondering how many women want to be conceited.

Natasha: Right. It's very fragile.

Deb: Contradictory at least.

Natasha: I think to have good self-esteem you have to have a balanced understanding of your own strengths and weaknesses. Self-esteem isn't without weakness.

Deb: Yes, and self-esteem isn't without strength. And I think we typically go to the opposite. Let me not show off all of my trophies because that would be conceited. To tell you that I've done, this, this, and this is conceit. But is it? Or is it just true?

Natasha: I struggle with that. I do carry with me a sense of humility that it's not appropriate to be blasting out my strengths, even to friends. To some extent I feel conscious about whether or not my discussion of strengths or what I've accomplished is going to be at the expense of somebody else. Whether or not promoting myself is at the expense of somebody else.

Deb: So we question, "How would they feel?" How would they feel, because you've done the work to accomplish a goal that they might feel bad about it? So why would you tell them about it?

Natasha: Yes.

Deb: Does that make sense that we would do that? Shouldn't they have their own strengths and accomplishments they could share as well?

Natasha: Yes, they should. I think with healthy social relationships, it's about encouraging people in their own strengths. I recognize that I worry how they would feel about themselves if I were to promote myself in any way.

Deb: Was there ever anybody in your life you can think back who gave you that perception, or felt that way themselves?

Natasha: My father is a humble man. It's almost as if he carries with him a presence. He doesn't need to tell who he is. He just is. And that's something that I carry with me.

Deb: I think you do carry a quiet sense of humbleness. I recognize humble, and yet I recognize smart, and I recognize those other things about you. I don't know. I wonder if we do a disservice to other individuals by discounting our greatness. And there is a difference between boasting and being proud of those things we've accomplished. Maybe that's where the difference is. I don't think you have to tell others about it, but I think you have to still feel worthy of everything.

Natasha: Day to day I'm aware of where I came from and who I was, and I think that is part of the comfort in who I am today. So I haven't forgotten it.

About Her Family

Deb: Can you tell me a little about where you came from, what you learned from your parents?

Natasha: I was raised by my father. He was the youngest son of a dairy farmer, and he had a lot of responsibility growing up. Very honest. There's nothing hidden by who he is. He doesn't talk about people. My parents were divorced when I was at a young age, and he's very careful even now about how he talks about my mother.

Deb: That's great.

Natasha: But he was not the kind of a man who communicated very well. Just as I said, he just is. So I found myself often struggling for his acceptance and validation. I'm more of an emotional person. My father just doesn't express it. So I think a lot of my sense of self-worth, I struggled in many ways. Wanting my father's support and validation, and encouragement but not really receiving it. My stepmother and I never really saw eye to eye. And I don't think I've had a strong female presence in my life. My mother is a proud woman, but she wasn't always consistent.

Deb: Talk a little bit about your father and the validation and acceptance. Do you feel like you've gotten it at this point?

Natasha: From him? I know he's proud of me, but I don't need him to tell me that. I think one of the changing points in my life was when I was around eighteen or nineteen and I came to realize that I was an "other validated" human being. I needed other people to tell me how worthy I was as a human being and I recognized I wasn't going anywhere.

Deb: That's awesome. How did you realize that? I know you're intelligent and I embrace that and think that's wonderful. Did you just realize it, or did something happen? Was it a shift?

Natasha: I was in therapy, and there was this one moment when he told me, "You are never going to change your parents. They are who they are." And it just was at the right time in my life to hear that. Also recognizing how easily I became devastated when things were going wrong in my life. Where a relationship was breaking up, or where I wasn't getting what I needed from somebody else, and it had dawned on me then: I need to figure out how to get that for myself.

Deb: How did you do that, and how do you get that from yourself now?

Natasha: It's still a process. It's recognizing that I need a sense of identity to understand who I am before I can have balance in the relationships that I have. I can't rely on them to really make me feel whole as a person. It's an important part of my life. I need these relationships in my life. I wouldn't be who I am without them, but I need that foundation. It's like the foundation of the house: The stones have to be well mortared to hold that foundation up. So it was through trial and error. It was recognizing I'm the only one who could be in control of what I'm thinking and not how anyone else was thinking.

Deb: So recognizing you were in control of it, and was it finding an identity?

Natasha: It was embracing what was already there. Accepting what was already there. As I said, I felt some discomfort and sometimes even embarrassment about my intelligence, but here it is. This is what got me through school. This is what allows me to be successful, and I need to embrace that.

About Her Body

Natasha: Also, other than the intelligence factor is my body. That is, I think becoming a mother was accepting a big part of who I was. Because here I was this young adult with a pretty well formed body and to allow another human being to be formed inside me to rip my body apart, to cause stretch marks and natural changes in my body and to realize that this is a wonderful thing to happen. I have this stretch mark. I don't want it, but it's there, and I have two sons to show for them. It's like a badge of honor versus something to want to get rid of. Definitely an acceptance of my body. Recognizing that having the right size breasts or being the right shape doesn't make a difference. Recognizing that so many beautiful women out there don't like themselves, don't like the way they look or want to look different and wonder what people think of them. So, I decided I didn't want that in my life anymore.

Deb: These are things that society tells women define, or don't define them. Women shouldn't be too smart and should focus on external beauty. It seems you accepted your body because you see the positive that it brought to you.

Natasha: Yes, my body has strength, has energy. It's what I need. It's not about forming your body to fit and then you'll be happy. That's never going to happen. My body is going to change, things are going to sag, and I'm going to go grey, going to get wrinkles. Beauty is a state of mind and not an external feature, although I still struggle with that at times.

Deb: Why do you think you would struggle with that or that any woman would struggle with that?

Natasha: It's an aspect of being wanted and being liked and being validated as being this outwardly beautiful human being. But through my experience in knowing people I think there's that sense of comfort. There's more than being outwardly beautiful that makes someone beautiful. And I recognize that from just talking with people and meeting people. I see beautiful people who are just torn apart from the inside, and it takes away from who they are. They carry themselves differently. They walk differently. They look around and are so aware of their external world because that's where they get their sense of value.

Deb: Again, society and media telling us what's acceptable. Models are getting thinner, and it's not reality. It's just not reality.

Natasha: I know people who have erroneously thought that if you're thin you have it all together, and that's just not the case. I've also felt embarrassed about talking about getting into shape, because people will look at me and say. "Why do you need to do that? You're so thin," but it's not about my size. It's about how I feel. I feel good when I'm strong.

Deb: So getting into shape doesn't mean getting thinner for you. It means feeling strong. Being able to lift your kids, being able to carry your groceries, being able to do the things you like to do because you're active.

What Would You Tell Young Women?

Deb: So, what would you like to say to your eighteen-year-old self?

Natasha: I think I would like to see support given to children to help them recognize their strengths and talents. Be supportive of them and not judgmental about them and to teach them to accept failure.

Deb: Yes, that's important.

Natasha: To learn how to adapt when things don't go well and just to create a supportive environment for them to become who they are.

Deb: And accept who they are. You have two boys. How are you going to do that with your boys?

Natasha: Part of what my father did with me rubbed off somehow. It wasn't an outward conversation; it was by him living an authentic life that helped me to learn to live an authentic life. I hope that for my sons. But I also hope to be supportive of them through their successes and their failures. It's just about accepting who you are.

Deb: You said "to support." What does that mean to you and is that to not only to be there, but also to be there with words, with hugs, with everything? Saying "Good job," "You tried you're best," "I'm proud of you anyway," right? Words are very powerful, and touch is very powerful, especially for children. Well, for all of us.

Natasha: Yes. A week ago, both of my boys entered an art contest for a local hardware store, and they had to draw this Easter picture. So my older son drew very nicely and stayed in the lines, and here my three-year-old is scribbling all over the paper. My three-year-old won the contest. It had to have been the cute factor, because, let's face it, it was a mess. I had to sit my older son down and explain to him that he didn't win the contest. And I found myself cringing about it because I felt that he deserved to win. But that's not realistic. So I sat my son down and explained that he joined the contest, and I was proud of him that he colored a beautiful picture, but that he did not win, and I had to sit with him while he cried.

Deb: And that could be enough.

Natasha: I wanted to protect him from it. I thought, "Why don't I go out and get him an Easter basket," because my three-year-old is going to be coming home with a basket, and I felt like I needed to stop myself.

Deb: Well that's what we do sometimes, with some team sports where everybody gets a trophy. There is some question as to whether or not that's good. Are we teaching kids that everybody wins?

Natasha: It's false. It's not an authentic sense of self. One thing my father I think did well is he let me fail.

Deb: How did he support you when you failed?

Natasha: He said another thing would come along.

Deb: That is accepting. Almost telling you, "Don't worry, you'll get the next one," and an expectation that you would keep trying. That not winning doesn't mean you give up.

Natasha: Yes.

On Humility and Self-Doubt

Deb: Just like I think there is a difference between self-esteem and self-conceit. I think there is a difference between being humble and being self-degrading. I think humility and humbleness are wonderful. I do think people don't have to tout [their accomplishments], but I also think that people shouldn't have to hide.

Natasha: I think I've been trying to balance between humility and self-defeat. It's hard to hear compliments. Even when I'm working with my clients well, it's hard to acknowledge that.

Deb: What makes that hard?

Natasha: It almost feels like you're capitalizing on somebody else's work. For me, there's something still missing there.

Deb: That's the piece we want to find, that's the piece. Is it possible that's your humility?

Natasha: I'm at the point of recognizing that and figuring out what to do with it. Am I struggling to be the most competent person out there and only when I feel like I'm the most competent person out there will I feel like I have hit the mark and I then can be satisfied? Is it because of that? I think that's partially true.

Deb: Where do you think that comes from? Why do you

have to be that? Can't you just be amazing and wonderful with the people you're with?

Natasha: I try to think of where that comes from, and I know my mother is somebody who is seemingly never satisfied. But I don't recall that ever being pushed on me.

Deb: Well, do we only learn by being told things?

Natasha: No, I think we learn by having things modeled for us.

Deb: Yes, so what kind of model did you get? It seems like you got, "I'm quiet in accomplishment" and "Accomplishment doesn't get you acknowledgment, so don't expect it."

Natasha: Don't expect acknowledgment.

Deb: Yet, all of us are worthy of acknowledgement, praise, honesty—especially from the people closest to us. To be worthy of it, yet comfortable enough in ourselves to not need it to validate us.

Natasha: To want acknowledgement, but not need it. That's exactly it.

Deb: And that's okay. It doesn't make you less humble. That makes you human.

Natasha: Right, but I think I grew up with mixed messages. My father is a man where you just do and you don't tout. My mother on the other hand. It's hard to put my finger on it, but it just seemed like it was never good enough. Like it's not good enough. You almost find yourself having a conversation in your head.

You hear something, and then you talk about it in [your head] and try to make sense of it.

Failure as Opportunity

Natasha: You know, I graduated with a master's degree in general theoretical psych and for a while worked in the field as a masters level counselor before I left the field for my kids. And when I came back, the law had changed and my degree was no longer eligible for licensure. I was, like, angry for a day, but it's the biggest lesson of my life. When I think failures, I think failures are opportunities, and if I wouldn't have gone back to school, I wouldn't have been back at the university, I wouldn't be in this program, wouldn't have been in the counseling center, which is probably one of the best experiences I've ever had.

Deb: You said you look at failure as an opportunity. It seems like we all have these conversations in our head.

Natasha: Whether you're aware of it or not. I think people would benefit from being mindful of those conversations. I wouldn't be here today if I wasn't mindful of what messages I am hearing/receiving and what messages I'm giving back.

Deb: So be mindful of it. Also, sounds like its normal for us to have this banter and to try, if we recognize we're being critical, to be more positive and look at a failure as, alright I'll feel sorry for myself for fifteen minutes and now I'm going to learn from this, take the opportunity and go.

Natasha: Stop running from the discomfort too, that it gives you. I think especially in this culture, we feel uncomfortable and we run from it. Anxiety is something we think we should not be feeling, really it's a healthy emotion to a degree anyway, because it tells you things and by listening to it, by sitting and experiencing that feeling rather than running from it, you can figure out what to do with it, and make good choices from it.

Deb: So sit with it, listen to your talk, don't wallow in it, but sit with it; don't push it away and see if it can help you.

Natasha: You wouldn't be writing this book if you didn't listen to it. Allowing yourself to experience discomfort and uncertainty.

Deb: Very true.

Natasha: For me acceptance has been through meaning. It's finding meaning through the struggles I've had. It's finding meaning through my successes. If you live the best way you can in that moment, there is no way you can't find meaning from what you do. And that includes the good, bad, and the 90 percent of your life that's in that gray area in between. It's okay to just be okay. And it's okay to have a bad day. It doesn't bring you down as a person, and it's also okay to shine.

Reflections

The media can make it difficult to age and feel good about oneself. Natasha, like so many of us, finds herself challenging those unrealistic images at times. Fortunately, she recognizes that they are unrealistic. She understands that being thin or physically attractive does not automatically equate to happiness. Natasha said she had poor self-esteem as a young girl, and she learned to embrace her strengths to build accomplishments leading to feelings of self-worth. Raised by a father she defines as humble, Natasha came to appreciate that trait. However, she recognizes there is some disparity between being humble and never talking about one's accomplishments or receiving praise. Natasha also reminds us that it's important to look at our "failures" as opportunities and to find meaning in our life experiences.

Introspection

Within you is the divine capacity to manifest and attract all that you need or desire.
-Wayne Dyer

Is self-esteem different from self-respect?

I believe they are different. Someone who lacks confidence may still very well value their life.
-Tammy G.

Self-esteem is when you are confident. Self-respect is when you have pride in yourself and what you do.
-Ruth O.

Yes, I know I am a good person, but that doesn't necessarily change the way I perceive myself regarding self-esteem.
-Melissa W.

I feel it is one in the same. Self-esteem is respecting oneself. Self-esteem is recognizing your self-worth and taking care of your own well-being.
-Linda C.

I think they overlap in definition and can sometimes be used interchangeably. Confidence, self-worth, pride, dignity...being self-assured and feeling like you are worth it!
-Janine O.

I do see a difference between the two. I don't think you can have self-esteem without self-respect, but I do think you can have self-respect without self-esteem. Self-esteem is a byproduct of self-respect.
-Diane F.

I think self-esteem is basically feeling comfortable in your own skin and self-respect is simply accepting who you are and liking yourself warts and all.
-Joanina L.

I think that they are synonymous.
-Christina D.

In a way I think it is, but I also think they tie together. Someone who has a low self-esteem is more likely to have a low self-respect for themselves. When someone has a low self-respect they are more likely to take part in unhealthy relationships and activities.
-Ashley W.

I feel it's connected. To me self-esteem is the way in which you think and feel about yourself. Self-respect to me is the way you treat yourself and allow others to treat you.
-Lacey T.

*I think self-esteem is what you believe about yourself,
mentally and emotionally. Self-respect is how you
portray that to others in your behavior and appearance.*
-Ann P.

Rose's Journey

I have come to the frightening conclusion that I am the decisive element. It is my personal approach that creates the climate. It is my daily mood that makes the weather. I possess tremendous power to make life miserable or joyous.
- Goethe

Every woman should have a friend like Rose. We have known each other since grade school, we went to college together, and years later found ourselves reconnecting in a hair salon that neither of us knew the other frequented. Whenever I think of her I can't help but smile because we laugh so much together. I think what attracted me to her spirit is Rose's genuine confidence in herself. She accepts herself and others simply as they are. She judges no one and doesn't accept others judging themselves when around her. Rose is an example of what I wish every child and adult would feel about themselves. She didn't grow into her self-confidence, she just has it. She is an inspiration to me, and I am fortunate to have her in my life.

Deb: Rose, you to me seem like you have always been confident. I think sometimes people present differently than we are, and I never felt that from you. I feel you are always authentic and comfortable with who you are. Has it always been like that for you?

Rose: I think it has been. At an early age, maybe I made that decision. I remember seeing different things that my father ended up doing in work. He was the head of [a union] for thirteen years, and he would have people calling at all sorts of hours. Saying one thing and turning around and doing another. You're supposed to be able to count on family and friends but often they can be the ones who take advantage. I decided a long time ago that I will give somebody one chance. They may not know I give them that chance. So I may end up just walking away from them if I feel that I've been slighted in a way where they have done something just evil, if they've done something bad to me or to those around me or my family. I've walked away from many situations, where I felt like I was not treated as I should be treated.

I'm not talking about a situation where you didn't call me, show up for dinner, or those things. I don't mean those types of slights. I mean they have to be major. Things that would cause either great dishonor, things people shouldn't do to each other, especially as friends. But I won't put myself in a position where I will get used and used and used. Because I saw that happen with my parents. You get one time, one chance with the big stuff.

You know the friend we went to school with, and over the years we were very close. Knowing her and her family, we were part of each other's lives for over twenty years. She put me in a position where I could have been in trouble with the law because of the choice she made, and she didn't consider how it might hurt me. I saw the issue through to get it cleared, and when it was resolved then had the conversation with her saying "Okay, we're done. We can't be friends ever again; I will not allow you to put me in this position again."

Deb: So you learned to stand up for yourself from your parents and experience. Because I think you are very forgiving, laid back and easy going. Not that people can push you, but that you accept and don't judge. So if people don't call that's fine, life happens. But you're saying that looking at your parents and how they were put in a bad position made you as an individual not want to be put into that position. There are so many women I think who would have trouble walking away from some people and relationships. So did your parents teach you that was okay? Did you just pick it up because you thought no way people will treat me like this because of my love for them? What prompted that?

Rose: I can't say. I had a very good childhood. I'm not saying that everything was perfect, but I had parents who stayed married, even though there were times when that didn't seem like it would happen. There was a time when one of my mother's friends tried to break up my parents; I mean I'm talking about the devious stuff. Those are the things you look at and then say to the person, "You are no longer part of my life."

Deb: And did your mother say that to her friend?

Rose: You know what, maybe. She didn't deal with her

anymore, for my mother that friend just didn't exist anymore. So maybe that's where I learned that.

Deb: Yeah. So it seems like your self-worth came from watching your parents saying, "I'm only going to take so much. We're good people, but you can only push us so far. We'll give you the shirt off our back, but when you try to steal it and hurt the people we love, we're done with you." So when it goes against your core and your values.

Rose: Your morals. You've got to have them, and I guess talking about it brings it up. It's not something I truly thought about before—it's just something I did. Seemed right, I guess. I didn't have people telling me what I was doing was right or wrong.

Deb: It seems like your family was always very supportive of you too, of you being who you were.

Rose: Absolutely, and it wasn't a household you got criticized in. I'm not saying that it didn't happen within the family. We have some negative people in the extended family. My grandmother would always criticize, and you would never hear the good stuff about people, only the bad. And I just have a hard time dealing with that. I never felt I had to say something negative about someone to make myself feel better.

Deb: To me, you're a great person; you have the huge heart. And you and your family open your heart, your lives, and give your love freely to other people. You also, as an individual, have worked your way up in your field, your career. It seems like you are confident. Have you always been confident in who you are as an individual?

Rose: I don't know that I've ever really explored it.

Deb: You just are?

Rose: There are days like, "Oh my God. Am I doing the right thing? How am I measuring up?" But for me that is a fleeting moment. I mean, I wasn't being told I was doing things wrong, or hurting people, so I guess I just took that and went with it.

Deb: So there was nothing other than you to contradict that you weren't good enough.

Rose: Right; and I wasn't going to beat myself up.

Deb: That's a great line, "I'm not going to beat myself up."

Rose: Well, yes. You know, I was always fat, the fat kid, but that didn't define me. So, I was the one on the playground standing up for the other fat kids and telling people to stop calling them names. Years later I had people from school saying thanks for doing that. I didn't think about it, I didn't know that it would affect them; all I know was it could have been one of my friends making the comment, and I would say "Stop that. It's not allowed here."

Deb: Well it seems like it's not one of your values or a value you want to be surrounded with.

Rose: There's no reason to drag somebody else down. If you're not feeling good about yourself, then go do something positive about it. I just didn't feel the need to lose the weight, I guess. [*Laughing*] I'm not going to beat myself up about it. So here I sit.

The Definition

Deb: When looking up the definition of self-esteem I found two definitions. One described a positive view of oneself and the other was "self-conceit." What do you think about self-esteem being defined as self-conceit?

Rose: I don't think I'm better than anyone else, but the thing is, I'm not looking for their approval. So, that wouldn't matter to me.

Deb: Was there ever a time when you looked for approval? Where you felt like you weren't enough? There doesn't have to be a "yes" here.

Rose: No, I'm thinking. Well it happened the other day. I thought, "Am I doing enough to help the team members in my stores to be more successful?" So that is doubting myself; doubting my expertise or ability to coach and provide expertise. So that [*pausing to think*] maybe went on for a day and a half off and on—not consistent. And it helped me by taking that time and taking that step back. It helped me put together a new way to tackle efficiencies with the team and coach a little better. So I kind of worked it out, worked it through.

Deb: So self-doubt doesn't have to mean self-degradation. What I'm hearing is that it doesn't mean "I'm not good enough," but "Am I doing enough?" And you're using self-doubt to make yourself better. To use it as an opportunity to say, "Well, maybe there is something, let me explore that." Not, "I'm probably not good enough."

Rose: Right.

Deb: But you don't dwell on this. Someone [with low self-esteem] might go home and say, "I must be doing something wrong. I must be a bad manager. I must be a bad leader." But that never crossed your mind.

Rose: It didn't.

Deb: That is awesome. So, any kind of criticism you've gotten, you haven't taken it personally. When I say personally, I mean you haven't gone and put a feeling to that criticism. You haven't said, "I feel bad because this person said this."

Rose: Right, because I think they are entitled to their opinion, and they need to voice their opinion. And how will it enrich my life if I react poorly to it?

Deb: You're an amazing woman; you're right. How will it enrich your life to hold on to it, especially if it makes you feel bad about yourself?

Rose: It works for the small things; it works for the large things. You have work life, you have home life, and you have [social] life. You have to be able to incorporate all of that.

Deb: I think there's a "mean girl" in so many of us that really is our worst critic. You have this great, wonderful philosophy. I think one of the reasons we are friends is that I was drawn to you and your confidence in who you are and your ability to just be who you are. You make me a better me by being with you. More confident in me and able to just be me and be accepted by me.

Rose: In the past, you mentioned some things that made me realize that other people didn't think the way I think. My manager says that to me as well. There are nine of us in our group, and she'll say if I open my mouth in a meeting it's usually in a way to calm the crowd. And to put a different twist on what they are asking us to do. I can usually see a different side of it that makes more sense. When people are saying, "How can I do this? There isn't time. There are only so many hours in a day, so many days a week. I need to have time with my family." Well [the company is not] asking us to do that, and we make a choice to do that. There are times when I work until midnight, but that's my choice, and it doesn't happen every day. Step back a little bit. If you stop the running and look at it, you can put it in perspective and get that calmer result.

Deb: And be just as effective.

Rose: Be more so.

Deb: And more confident in yourself if you're not taking on that responsibility. How about at home?

Rose: With [my husband], we don't fight. Usually people fight over money matters. But I think you should pick your battles. I'll ask, "Are we supposed to do anything tonight? Deb can do dinner." He says, "Go have a good time," If he said no, then first, I would be like, "You better have a damn good reason to say that."

Deb: Yes, in a healthy relationship, you aren't defined by the other person, but enhanced by the other person.

Rose: Some people would never dream of doing things apart, whereas, we do take vacations apart, and that's a good thing, not an anxiety thing. He can go hunting; I can go to the beach. Life is good.

Deb: You both come back and can be even better for it.

Rose: Yes, and that's us. It doesn't work for everybody. I can probably count on one hand the actual number of real arguments. Really it's a debate; just where "I can't talk to you now." He is different when he goes with his family and comes back. It's like they all go back to that childhood yelling at each other. Why are you yelling? To them it's a conversation; to me they are screaming at each other. That doesn't happen with us, it just doesn't. So I'll be like, "I understand where this [yelling] is coming from, and you have to work through that stuff. And now you're really upset with them, and you work that out." I'm also not going to instigate that. If he needs down time, relax, whatever you need to do. Am I going to ask him to do a chore around the house, no? Again, pick the battles. I don't care what we were supposed to do after that, no way.

Deb: It's recognizing your partner's needs too.

What Would You Tell Young Women?

Deb: What would you tell young women, or women of any age, who might not feel really good or might not have a strong self-worth, might not feel good about who they are?

Rose: I mean, the only thing that comes to mind real fast is "Why?", "Why not?" That's tough for me, Deb, because you need to be able to put yourself first but also be there for those you care about. You have to be able to protect yourself. And sometimes that might be moving away or staying away from certain people. To see what happens to me when I am away and when I don't have this other person in my ear with a criticism. You're going to have to decide if that [criticism and relationship] is going to define you. Should it, and will it make you better? How will it make you stronger and not pull you down?

Deb: Yeah, not to hold on to it. Like you said earlier, you had a great quote, "I'm not going to beat myself up."

About Her Mother

Rose: I didn't realize growing up that my mother's parents were divorced.

Deb: You didn't know?

Rose: We didn't discuss it. How do you bring it up? We didn't really see them. They lived [out of state]. My mother's mother was having an affair, and she left the husband and the kids.

Deb: And your mother was raised by . . . ?

Rose: Her father's mother. She was the oldest of the five kids. You can see what it took for her to do what she needed to do.

Deb: So did she leave? Was leaving her answer to get away from that?

Rose: She met my dad who was in the army, and she was seventeen. They got married and came back here to get married. He was actually engaged. So there're a lot of things in the past, but I wouldn't have known that. The different things my mother had to do to care for her siblings, she didn't make that a burden.

Deb: We all have something, so don't make it a burden.

It doesn't have to define you; you can define yourself.

Rose: I do really think it helps mold you.

Deb: Yes.

Rose: Everything in your past it can either be that great foundation, that sturdy rock, or it can be the slab that buries you.

Deb: Yes, so it's the way I/we interpret it. So, if I choose to accept what's handed to me and make lemonade out of lemons, instead of sitting there and being sour about it and feeling sorry for myself, I could have a different life. Either way I will have a different life.

Rose: And it's a lot easier for me to say because I did have parents who didn't knock me down. They didn't knock me down verbally. They didn't say, "I can't believe you're doing that." You know, they were not negative to me or around me.

Deb: That is such a gift; you should know that is such a gift.

Rose: Yes, I was very, very fortunate. I've often said I've led a sheltered life.

Deb: Well they protected you, but they didn't shield you from going out and stumbling yourself either. So sheltered in what ways? It seems they gave you just enough freedom to make your own mistakes and build your own self-confidence and self-worth. And to know that it didn't matter what you tried, but that you would be loved and worth something regardless of whether you succeeded or failed.

Rose: And I didn't have to think about that. That's what makes it different. There's a lot of people out there who had to do a lot more to feel good about themselves.

Deb: Yes.

Rose: For them to realize they weren't a bad kid. They didn't do horrible things. But if you're constantly hearing the negative, what more can you think?

Deb: Yes, and it's so unfortunate.

Rose: Sometimes it's the unspoken word. It's almost if you don't say anything you give people permission to try to figure it out themselves. And sometimes that person you are trying to coach or parent, they don't know that they can question those negative words.

Deb: You're right. Kids don't know, which is why parents can play such a big role. We are defined by where we come from. But as an adult we get to decide which pieces I keep. Which pieces do I like? Which values of my family do I like? So if your family is Catholic you get to decide, "I'm not going to be Catholic." If your family only eats ravioli on Christmas, you can decide to eat turkey instead. You get to make decisions big and small, but you have to feel like you deserve to make decisions big and small. And we typically look at the people around us, so there are some people who may be assertively saying "You're worthless." And there are others just by their actions, mothers and fathers, who by not acting strong, make us feel like, I'm worthy, *but.* It's that "but" that we can change.

Reflections

Rose admits having it easier than some by growing up in a household where she was never criticized. She chooses to not be around people who do not treat her as she feels she should be treated. When asked what she would say to young girls who don't feel good about who they are, Rose basically responds with "What purpose are you getting from feeling bad?" If there is an opportunity to grow from feedback, then take it and grow, but then let it go. If there is no growth opportunity, what's the point in holding onto that criticism? She explains she has no intention of beating herself up, as there seems to be no point in it. So, she chooses not to. It's a great attitude, and one I wish that many may come to adopt. Talking negatively about others wasn't something Rose ever found helpful. She suggests that if people don't feel good about themselves, they should do something about it, instead of putting other people down. I like her "What's the point?" attitude about holding onto negative criticism is a wonderful philosophy. What *is* the point? Is there any answer that wouldn't tell us to let it go?

Introspection

Do your thing, do it unapologetically. Don't be discouraged by criticism. You probably already know what they're going to say. Pay no mind to the fear of failure. It's far more valuable than success. Take ownership, take chances, and have fun. And no matter what, don't ever stop doing your thing.
–Asher Roth

What words of wisdom do you have for younger girls/women about self-esteem?

Be true to yourself. Follow your gut instincts. Learn from your mistakes. Keep your mind, body and soul in balance. Take time for yourself. Take time to be still.
-Tammy G.

Don't be in a hurry to grow up. Take pride in yourself.
-Ruth O.

To be a strong person—being a leader allows you to feel confident about yourself. It is important to love

119

yourself. We all have strengths and weaknesses.
-Melissa W.

Respect yourself by expecting to be treated with respect. Respect yourself by taking care of yourself—do what is good for your well-being. Don't be afraid to let your voice be heard and to express your opinion. Recognize that everyone has strengths and weaknesses and gifts from God. Concentrate on your strengths and don't be too hard on yourself when it comes to your weaknesses. Do your very best and always keep your self-respect. Focus on the gifts that God has given you and do your best to share them with others.
-Linda C.

Just try your best to do things that you really enjoy and use your talents to their fullest. Find a great hobby that brings you joy. Don't give up on things you really want to accomplish. Don't put any merit on individuals that have negative comments and harsh words about your dreams. I wish everyone was able to have parents like mine, but if they don't, hopefully they can benefit from a good role model, teacher or mentor. Try to surround yourself with individuals that are happy and upbeat and eager to learn and have fun. Notice how you feel when you are around certain people. At times, negative and depressing people can bring you down and cause you to fall into that same mode. Avoid those types. Use your surroundings at home and outside to tap into nature and all living things. I find the environment, wildlife and music to be very uplifting and bring good energy to the soul. Visualize how you want to be and take steps to achieve it.
-Janine O.

Always educate yourself. Self-improvement, self-study. Education is so important. Learning new things for

both career and personal development is so healthy.
-Diane F.

Time and life teaches many lessons. Just try to be the best you can be. And then, more importantly, be content inside yourself. You are a worthy person and always will be.
-Joanina L.

Always respect yourself because if YOU don't, then why should anyone else? Don't rely on someone else for your happiness and self-worth. Only you can be responsible for that. If you can't love and respect yourself—no one else will be able to make that happen. Accept who you are completely—the good and the bad—and make changes as YOU see fit, not because you think someone else wants you to be different.
-Christina D.

Never compare yourself to someone. Everyone has their own way to do things and their own way of thinking. The longer you compare yourself to someone or to standards in society the longer it takes for you to find your true identity.
-Ashely W.

Always trust your gut. If you have a dream you should try everything possible to achieve it before it slips away.
-Ann P.

The Ending is Just the Beginning

Do not wish to be anything but what you are,
and try to be that perfectly.
-St. Francis De Sales

How might we improve self-esteem in ourselves and others? Below are a few suggestions, based on my own experience and the experience of the other women featured in this book. As you read the stories of these women did you recognize some themes? Themes that included needing life experience to gain confidence, challenging yourself to accomplish things that will help you develop that confidence and finding support from those around us to help us see the truly amazing people we are. They have also suggested that we encourage and celebrate each other's accomplishments, refrain from judgment, and accept each other for the gifts we each offer. We can also begin recognizing that self-esteem is not equal to self-conceit. Just as the women I interviewed, you can be humble and still be accomplished, proud and confident. Let's consider this a starting point for more conversations that encourage and enhance self-esteem in all of us.

Change Our Perception

We may not be able to change the definition of self-esteem overnight, but we can change our interpretation of it. How? First by recognizing that self-esteem is not conceit. If we think that any sharing of accomplishments is considered conceit, we will hide these pieces of ourselves. It is actually in accomplishing that we build our self-esteem and recognize our capabilities. But if we are embarrassed by and hide our successes, we limit our ability to grow our self-esteem. We begin to believe these accomplishments were "not a big deal." This untrue belief further chips away at our self-esteem.

Think of developing self-esteem as being equal to a great cake you baked. If, each time you mix the batter, you question if it's done right and throw it in the garbage, the cake will never get in the oven to bake. Each time we throw away the batter, we lose faith we can ever have a piece of cake. Similarly, each time we throw away an accomplishment, we get stuck in a space that doesn't allow for us to fully experience that good feeling inside that helps us know that we are capable. By the way, there are some great bakeries out there with awesome cake, just as there are great people out there who will be happy to help you achieve and bask in your successes. Stop denying yourself that feeling of accomplishment—big and small. They are all important ingredients in your recipe for developing positive self-esteem.

How else to change our perception? We can find role models and listen to other women's success stories. The women in this book share some wonderful experiences. They were not bragging or boastful, but honest in the ups and downs of their life experiences. As you read the stories of these women, did you see conceit or humility? As others share their accomplishments with us, let's celebrate in them, recognizing that we are adding to their own recipe for successful development of self-esteem.

Be Kind to Yourself and to Others

Embrace the fact that we are all unique people. You cannot be me. I cannot be you. We can try to learn from each other, emulate behaviors, but we cannot be anyone but ourselves. Should a person feel bad if she gets a job and another doesn't? Should I feel bad if you get the job and I do not? Am I a worthless human being because I didn't get the job? No, but if my self-talk is negative, then I will begin to feel like a useless and worthless human being.

Let's change the way we define self-esteem and allow each other to bask in our accomplishments. Let's pick people up and remind them of their positives, especially when all they can see are their negatives. If your best friend came to you and said she didn't get a job she wanted would you say, "Well that's because you wore the wrong clothes, or you said stupid things, or you aren't worthy of good jobs." Not a chance! You would tell her, "The right one is waiting around the corner. You are amazing and any company would be lucky to have you. You are worthy of a good job."

What about those people who aren't our best friends? In their stories, MJ and Laura agree that there is a need to accept each other for all the talents and differences we possess. Let's try to notice when we are being judgmental and stop ourselves when we are judging others. This can be difficult because, wherever you turn, the media is talking about how someone put on weight, chose the wrong hair color or didn't wear the dress as good as someone else. Who cares? Really. Who cares if you and I wore the same dress, and you chose black shoes and I chose red? Who cares?

The only one who should care is *me*. Maybe I like the red shoes. Maybe they remind me of someone. Maybe I just broke the heel on my black shoes that morning. Who cares? Really, in the grand scheme of things, do you really think I should give a damn about what you think about my shoes? What if you learned I gave my black shoes to a charity? What if I have twenty pairs of black shoes and just wanted to wear the red ones? Does that make me a bad person? Should I go home and think that I'm stupid, ugly, or worthless? No. Let's make a conscious effort to build people up with compliments and positive statements.

Stop the comparisons. The media encourages us to be robots—all looking, acting, dressing, and thinking alike. Would you go to an ice cream parlor that serves only one flavor? What a dull world this would be if we were all alike. Don't become a robot or encourage the making of more robots.

Be A Mentor

Mentor the young as well as our peers. Many people we know can use a boost. Let's start giving them just that. Be free with compliments and don't assume people know their talents. Many women may not know they are smart, funny, or intuitive. They may be acting. So, let's help them recognize and accept the amazing person we see.

Providing positive feedback, compliments and encouragement even in failures can help build resilience: the ability to bounce back easily from challenges. We learn that it's okay to fall, so long as we get back up. I don't know any parents who would yell at their infant who keeps falling as he learns to walk. Each time the baby falls, the parent runs over and helps the child up while providing words of support and encouragement. The same is true as you teach a child to ride a bike. If she falls off the first time, do you yell at her? No, you pick her up, dust her off and say, "Okay, let's try it again." It's no different than being passed over for the job you wanted. Pick yourself up, dust yourself off, and move forward feeling confident you can try again.

Where's The Proof?

If I say you are worthy, your first thoughts might be "Yes, of course, everybody's worthy." Then you may think to yourself, "Except when I do this" or "I would be more worthy if I did that." There is no need to challenge the thought. It's true: You are worthy. Worthy of a good life, food on your table, a healthy relationship, and almost anything else that your heart desires. Building self-esteem can be difficult when our internal dialogue constantly criticizes our choices and flaws and even pokes at our strengths.

It's important to challenge that inner critic. Make sure it's being reasonable and not hurtful. Make sure the feedback is true and not filled with lies based on old beliefs. One thing I like to ask my clients to do is find the proof. If you say "I'm worthless," where's the proof? And then ask if there is proof to the contrary. If you get a 60 on a test and think you are stupid, is that really true? Maybe you didn't study. Maybe it's a subject you hate. Do you always get 60s, even when you like the subject and study? Where's the true proof that you are stupid? Just because your father might have said you're stupid when you were five, does that mean it's true?

How do you stand up to the critic? The first

step is to notice the positive or negative self-talk you may have. What is your critical voice saying to you? Next, recognize you have the power to talk back. Most of us just accept these thoughts and assume they are truths. What if the critical voice is lying to you? What if you actually are smart, funny, beautiful and amazing? What if the truth is you are worthy—as worthy as anyone else in the world? How would you live your life if you felt worthy? Would you expect more from yourself and from those around you? Would you apply for better jobs, engage in conversation without questioning your intelligence or expect respect from your partner?

Does that mean you won't have self-doubt? No. You will. There have been many times in my life—and I'm sure there will be many more—where I question whether or not I did the right thing, made the right choice and so on. However, these are opportunities to learn, not to criticize. Self-doubt can be healthy as it will help us prepare to tackle whatever goals we set for ourselves, or at the very least assist in us putting our best foot forward. As a matter of fact, Ruth and Natasha talk about self-doubt as something that drives and motivates them to do things better. It doesn't stop them from trying and succeeding.

Final Note

There are too many women out there today who are absolutely amazing who do not believe in themselves. Is your experience similar to mine, thinking you are the only one in the room who feels inferior? What if it's your daughter, best friend, mother or sister? What if it's your niece, favorite teacher or coach who thinks she is "less than"? I'm here to tell you it is so. I sit across from many women who do not see their own amazing spirit. They are beating themselves up every

day for simply being human. It's time to stop. There is
no reason for a woman to think she isn't beautiful,
capable, wonderful, and worthy.

There are many factors that play into our self-
esteem: our childhood, past beliefs, negative comments
from others, and society's depiction of and expectations
of women. We can't change our histories, but we can
impact our future. It's time to embrace self-esteem as a
positive personality trait, and not something to be
hidden and ashamed of. With some self-reflection and a
shift to a positive perception of self-esteem, we can
begin to accept ourselves more fully, flaws and all.
Understanding that mistakes are opportunities to learn
instead of failings can help us to move confidently
toward the goals we set for ourselves without fear of
"hurting" others' feelings or being considered conceited.

I am so grateful for the women who have
contributed to this book with their journey's and by
answering the questionnaires. I can tell you each one is
amazing, accomplished, smart, funny, and each has
unique gifts and talents. They are 100 percent perfect as
themselves. These are not their words, but mine.
Because the truth is they are not conceited, but humble
and modest as they share their accomplishments. Now
it's your turn to move forward in the understanding
that you a capable and worthy human being. It's time to
find your true voice and talk back to the critic within.
It's time to stand up and say to that critical voice,
"Sorry, I'm not interested in hearing you bash me. I
wouldn't let you bash my best friend, and I love myself
at least as much as I love her. So back up and hit the
road. I'm done with you."

Let the conversations begin!

NOTES

Chapter: Defining Self-Esteem

1. Self-esteem. (n.d.). In *Merriam-Webster Dictionary* online. Retrieved from http://www.merriam-webster.com/dictionary/self-esteem.

2. Self-esteem. (n.d.). *Dictionary.com Unabridged.* Retrieved from http://dictionary.reference.com/browse/self-esteem.

3. Self-esteem. (n.d.). *Collins English Dictionary.* Retrieved from http://www.collinsdictionary.com/dictionary/english/self-esteem?showCookiePolicy=true

4. Self-esteem. (n.d.). *Collins American English Dictionary.* Retrieved from http://www.collinsdictionary.com/dictionary/american/self-esteem?showCookiePolicy=true

5. Mruk, C.J. , & O'Brien, E.J. (2013). Changing Self-esteem through Competence and Worthiness Training: A Positive Therapy. In V. Zeigler-Hill (Ed.), *Self-Esteem* (163). New York: Psychology Press.

6. Mayo Clinic Staff. (July 23, 2011). *Self-esteem Check: Too Low, Too High or Just Right?* Retrieved from http://www.mayoclinic.com/health/self-esteem/MH00128/NSECTIONGROUP=2.

7. Branden, N. (2013.) *Healthy Self Esteem*. Retrieved from http://www.nathanielbranden.com/discussions/self-esteem/healthy-self-esteem/. (Reprinted with permission.)

8. Pyszczynski, T., & Kesebir, P. (2013). Existential perspective on the need for self-esteem. In V. Zeigler-Hill (Ed.), *Self-Esteem* (133). New York: Psychology Press.

9. Branden, N. (2010). The psychology of self-esteem: A revolutionary approach to self-understanding that launched a new era in modern psychology. (32nd ed.). New York: Jossey-Bass.

ABOUT THE AUTHOR

Deb Pavlico is a Licensed Professional Counselor in the state of Pennsylvania. She is a member of the American Counseling Association and Pennsylvania Counseling Association.

Counseling is a second career for Deb who has worked in community mental health and at the Counseling Center at Marywood University. She remains part-time at Marywood and has a private practice in Kingston, Pennsylvania.

Prior to her returning to school, Deb worked in operations, customer service and various leadership roles in a Fortune 500 company. She has an M.S. in Community Counseling from the University of Scranton and a B.S. in Business Administration from Wilkes College.

36123776R00084

Made in the USA
Lexington, KY
07 October 2014